So You Want to be a Landlord?

SAMUEL R. SILIGATO III

DEDICATION

I would like to dedicate this book to my wife Sherry, whose patience has seen me through the rental business, whose love I have cherished for almost thirty years, and whose life I will share through our retirement years together.

CONTENTS

ACKNOWLEDGMENTS

I want to thank Dr. Mary Ann Diorio for the initial edit of this book and helpful comments. It was through her encouragement that I began to write many years ago.

Not enough can be said for the help my daughter Jean has been in the final preparations of "So You Want To Be A Landlord". Hours and hours of editing, re-writes, and preparing the various computer formats, have enabled me to get to this point. Without her help, 'Dad' would be lost.

Finally, thanks to my wife and two other daughters Faith and Samantha. They sacrificed countless hours as Dad 'worked the business'---preparing and renting various properties. I Love You!

DISCLAIMER

This book was written to provide reliable information concerning the investment real estate business. The author is not engaged in rendering financial or legal advice. Each investor should check with local and state laws concerning investing in one's particular state as laws do vary, and should check with local attorneys and accountants as needed. The author disclaims any liability that might be incurred from any application of the book's contents.

INTRODUCTION

SO YOU WANT TO BE A LANDLORD was written to benefit those of you who are contemplating the possibility of becoming a landlord, and those who may already be in the business but are interested in finding that "extra nugget" that could make your business more profitable. This book will accomplish both of these objectives.

At the time of this writing, I have been a landlord for 17 years, dealt with countless tenants, seen the rewarding side of the rental business, and experienced the low, humbling side as well. It would have been great had I had someone who would sit down with me and try to prepare me for what has occurred over the last seventeen years. I "went to school" on my first few properties, and had I been advised beforehand, my "lessons" would have been less expensive.

Upon graduation from college, I thought that my future was set, and that I knew what I would be doing for the next twenty years or so. I earned my teaching degree, taught for a total of six years, then found myself involved in sales of retail furniture. I managed the business for eighteen years before finally leaving to work the rental business full time. Ten years or so into the retail business, the thought occurred that I could be spending the rest of my life here, and while the pay was not bad, when it came time for retirement, I would be left out in the cold. If the business should fail or cease to be, I would walk out the door with no pension or security for future years. Had this occurred at an age that might be considered too old to start over again, I would be left at the mercy of Social Security, and any savings that I could accumulate over the years. There is good reason to question whether or not Social Security will be available in 20 years and beyond. How would I be able to pay for three college educations and marry off my three daughters on what I could save? Simple. I couldn't!

Soon panic set in, and I needed to find another vehicle to accomplish the goals in my future. Investing in real estate seemed to have the potential to acquire both short-term and long-term income. I did not know anything about investing in rental properties, but ideally, and on paper, it seemed like a worthwhile endeavor. My first venture was with a group of friends. Five of us purchased a four-unit apartment building. I learned many valuable lessons from that experience. After that, and ever since, I have been on my own, leaving my full time job many years ago. I have acquired several rentals, purchased, renovated, and re-sold several more. I have chosen properties for the long term and short term, and sold rentals when the 'time was right'.

If you are ready to plunge in for the first time, you will find, in the pages to follow, both sides of the story to help you make up your mind. The landlord business is not for everyone, but it can be your ticket to prosperity. You don't become successful overnight, and as I will mention several times, this business is a process, not a get rich quick scheme.

Should you decide to be a landlord, I feel that it is imperative that you set out with specific goals in mind that establish a time frame and definite financial objectives. The goals can and will be changed and adjusted as you journey through the "process". When I teach seminars on this subject, I always tell the classes that "being a landlord is a business with potential I would wish on all of my friends, and with headaches I wouldn't wish on any of them". There's no question the potential IS THERE! That's why I am in the business. Short term, I have been able to use the generated income to allow me to leave my full-time job. Long term, the sale of these properties will pay for college educations, weddings, and finally retirement.

CHAPTER 1

WHY DO YOU WANT TO BE A LANDLORD ANYWAY?

We all have reasons for the things we do. Before we get into the landlord business, we should all have some very good reasons. Some of these reasons do not include wanting to get calls in the middle of the night because the heater is not working or the roof leaks. Nor do they include wanting to put up with tenants that do not take care of your property or wanting to get involved with their numerous personal difficulties. Such difficulties often lead to their reasons, justified or not, for their not being able to pay the rent on time. Certainly none of us wants to become a landlord so that we are in a position to pay more city, state, and federal taxes. Don't worry, you will have this opportunity whether you want it or not. Why, then, would anyone want to subject himself to the problems and headaches of being a landlord?

The answer of course is to make money. How much you make is totally up to you and will be a result of the time and effort that you put into the business. Can you "Get Rich Quick"? Possibly, but this is certainly the

exception to the rule. Perhaps you have seen one of the many individuals

who advertise their courses on real estate investment, and how, with

seemingly little effort, have amassed hundreds of thousands of dollars in real

estate in a short time. Am I saying that this doesn't happen? No. It could,

but the percentage is extremely small. It may cost you hundreds of dollars to

learn someone's particular technique. If it works, it is absolutely worth the

investment. If it happens to you—wonderful! I am involved with the

"process" of the business, and over time, I will accomplish the goals I have set

for myself and my family.

Many of the courses I have seen offer ways to obtain real estate with very

little or nothing down. They also tell you how to leverage properties to

purchase others and how to find properties that owners will trade for or hold

mortgages. These things do happen, but most of the time, you need to have a

track record in real estate, have money or a bank already behind you, and be

extremely lucky to find the deals that some courses speak of. This book is a

hands-on approach for the beginner, and in the chapters that follow, you will

learn of the trench experiences that you may come against. There is plenty of

money to be made in real estate, but you will have to work for it. Part of the

'process' of being in the investment business is learning how to work 'smarter

and not harder" over the years. You will learn how to avoid potential

problem properties and choose those which will give you the greatest return.

However, if you are looking to get into the landlord business for the exclusive reason of making money, you will miss some of the more rewarding aspects of the business as well as "key" ingredients necessary to become a successful landlord. The landlord business allows you to be your own boss, which, in itself, has many benefits. Running your own business has responsibilities as well. In years past, and I hope, still today, business was a service to the public. Owners provided goods or services to benefit the community; the best service for the best possible price. As a landlord, you, too, have a service that will benefit the community, and if you are to be a truly successful landlord, you need to recognize the fact that you are a servant as well as your own boss. You will need to take care of your property and your tenants. Tenants are not only people, but they are your customers. These customers will be the ones paying for and supporting your business over the years. Be determined to give the best possible product for the best possible price. You will be rewarded with tenants who take care of your property and pay you faithfully. Sure, there will be exceptions, but overall, your service to them will earn you respect and success in every facet of the business.

Another measure of satisfaction that I gain is the feeling of achievement and self-satisfaction that comes as a result of taking a property that is not very appealing and turning it into a nice, clean, apartment or home. It makes me feel good to see the results of my work. It gives me a sense of satisfaction to provide a good place to live for the tenants and families to whom I rent.

CHAPTER 2

SETTING GOALS

What goals should you be setting? The answer depends on you and what you expect to accomplish in a given time period. Are you looking for something "extra" to do in your spare time? Do you see this business as a means of savings, perhaps to finance an education or build a new home in future years? Do you see this as a means for leaving your present job and providing a way of retirement?

Maybe you don't know how far you want to go at this time. It has been said that owning just one property can 'eat you alive.' At first, I did not understand what this meant, but one property, especially a single family residence, seems to have a way of chewing up any extra cash flow you might realize. To get into this business just to fill some spare time is probably not the way to go. If you find that perfect property, then perhaps just one property will suit you just fine. If it becomes one that needs constant attention, you may find yourself cursing the day that you bought it. We will discuss more about different properties in future chapters.

The rental business can be an excellent way to save for future, expensive items that will be needed such as a wedding, college education, or new home. You may not actually see the money flowing into your pocket on a monthly basis, but the equity that you accumulate over the years has a way of sneaking up on you, and before you know it, you have a property that is paid for. You will have the option to sell and pocket most of the money (less what you pay in taxes) or continue to rent and not pay a mortgage payment every month.

Real estate/rental business can be a vehicle for retirement. You can attain a very good retirement income from the properties you acquire over the years, or the business could become your livelihood. When I started, I still had to work my regular job. There were many evenings and weekends that were spent getting properties in shape to rent, re-painting, cleaning and repairing when tenants moved out. I also began to purchase properties that I could re-sell once they were renovated. In most cases, they were properties that needed a good deal of work and much time. I could have chosen to hire others to do the work, but that would have created a cash problem, and then the resulting profit would be such that the venture did not benefit me. Since I chose to do much of the work myself, I was required to spend my free time getting my hands dirty, not to mention the time that I was forced to spend away from my wife and three young daughters. You have to ask yourself if it is really worth your time and effort. There were times that my wife made it very clear that she was not having a good time when I was out working on the properties. Men, and women for that matter, must remember to keep a proper balance. Lost time with your family can never be made up.

I have approached the business with the following perspective. In my mind, I envisioned buying properties with an average value of say $50,000 to $100,000 each. If, at the end of fifteen years, that property would be paid for, I would have gained that much of equity. I then projected what I thought I would need to pay for three college educations and three weddings. That should be a mere 6 billion! No, it's not quite that bad, but you will be surprised how those expenses can add up. Each family's need is different, so you will project according to your needs. Also, I determined the amount I thought sufficient for my future needs and retirement. This amount would allow me to live comfortably and permit me to make the choice as to how I spend my time. I intend on spending retirement with my family, doing things that I *want* to do. Once I had a general figure in mind, let's say for the sake of example, $500,000, I determined that I would need 10 properties that average $50,000 each. My goal would be to acquire these properties as soon as possible and try to have them paid off within a fifteen-year period. Theoretically, within 20 to 25 years, I would have a half million dollars waiting for me as I needed it. As I mentioned, plans and goals can and will be changed according to circumstances, needs, and desires. At this point, it is simply important to get pointed in the right direction with a general game plan. You may choose properties with higher values, fewer properties, less properties, hold them for shorter periods, whatever. As you acquire properties, there may be some that you want to get rid of, undesirable for whatever reason, some you may decide to keep even after they are paid for, and some you may want to pass on to your children. The scenarios are endless, but we will have a plan, and we will bend it, change it, enhance or cancel it, as time goes by. The object is to formulate a plan.

CHAPTER 3

GETTING STARTED

As with most long term goals or projects, one of the most difficult, if not *THE* most difficult step, is the first step. To take that plunge is hard to do. Your life will change to some degree or another because of your choice. Uncertainty, fear of the unknown, the risk factor, all seem to team up against you to prevent you from getting involved. These feelings are not to be totally ignored. Sometimes the decision to become a landlord is not the right one. Sometimes one would be better off investing money in a CD or money market account where it will be safe and cozy and not call in the middle of the night to say that there is a problem. It takes a certain kind of bird to be a landlord, and if your gut is telling you *NO WAY,* then maybe you should listen. By the same token, whenever a new venture comes along, there is always a degree of anxiety. Don't be intimidated. Most people do not get into the landlord business because they know little or nothing about the business and buying properties, or they just don't know how to manage properties. Managing properties is a learning experience as well. You will make mistakes just like the rest of us. The key is to learn from mistakes and not repeat them.

You may have heard that it takes money to make money. Unless you have other property to use as leverage against the next property that you want to purchase, to some degree you will need to come up with funds for the purchase and/or closing of your investment property. So where does this money come from? If you have a substantial amount saved, you might consider using this as your startup capital. This is a good source if available, but remember, there is a cost to you for this money as well. It may not be as high a cost as borrowing from a bank, but you will be risking the interest at least that you will have earned in whatever savings account you use. A general rule is that most institutions will require 20% down on investment properties and may ask a higher rate of interest than if you were purchasing the property as your primary residence. In a future chapter, I will discuss ways in which you can lessen this amount.

Types of bank loans are Conventional (20% down), FHA (Government backed-loans usually with a lower amount required down and lower interest rates), and the Commercial loan (usually an interim loan). You will be required to pay an application fee, usually $350 or so, points, which could vary from one to three. Points are a percentage of the loan amount. For example, if you were required to pay one point on a $60,000 loan, the amount would be

$600. Two points equals $1200, and three points would total $1800. These fees are to be paid at the time of closing. Sometimes lending institutions call the points by other names such as loan origination fees or commitment fees. A fee is a fee is a fee. Sometimes the commitment fee is due upon your acceptance of the mortgage commitment. Often, these fees are non refundable should you decide not to go through with the loan.

Other costs you may encounter with a loan or mortgage will be the survey ($300-500), and title insurance on the property you plan to purchase. The fee for title insurance is determined by the amount of the purchase you are making. On a property for sale at $60,000, the title work and insurance should be around $500 to $600. Attorney review fees are fees that attorneys charge to review all the paperwork involved in the transaction and may include fees to draw up particular documents.

Your personal credit history can do wonders one way or the other. If you have good or excellent credit, you will have many more financial doors open to you. If your credit rating is not good, then you will have a difficult time in your quest. If you do have questionable credit rating, you would be wise to take a few months at least to 'clean up' any outstanding problems. Perhaps you could consolidate several smaller loans which would give you one payment rather than five or six. If you are not able to consolidate, begin to pay off your delinquent credit. I would suggest writing down your bills listing them from smallest to largest. Plan to pay the minimum on each bill but the smallest. Pay off the smallest bill, then work toward paying off the next smallest. Continue this until the bills are all current and manageable. Once you have a track record of six to twelve months of current payments, you will be in a much better position to talk with lenders about your investment property.

One problem I ran into when I started was that I did not have a "track record" with investment properties. The first few institutions that I approached all said that I had a good idea, my credit was okay, BUT, since I did not have a history in the rental business, they would not be able to help me at this time. However, each of them said to come back to see them once I had a few properties. Thanks a lot! Well, once I could get to the position of holding several properties, I would not need them, so it wasn't likely that I would be back. Finally, my first two properties were purchased with short-term commercial loans which were converted to regular mortgages once the properties were renovated and rented. At that point, banks were likely to be willing to place a regular mortgage on the property for me. As the number of my properties increased, it was easier to get the money necessary for the next project. Did I get approved every time I went to get a mortgage in the beginning? No. I continued to try until I found someone who would help.

I know of individuals who have purchased properties on credit cards. I don't recommend this approach, but if there are no other alternatives, it may be the way to go for the short term. Interest rates on credit cards are usually much too high for the long term. Sometimes properties may be in such disrepair that lending institutions will not lend you money. If the house is inexpensive enough, you might consider a credit card until the property is renovated. Then you will be in a much better position to obtain a mortgage or home equity loan on the property.

The home equity loan is an excellent tool to acquire properties. If you own your home or have enough equity built up to take out a home equity loan, you can use these funds to purchase properties, renovate and rent them, then take out a home equity loan or mortgage on your investment property and use those funds to pay off the equity loan on your home. There are several types of home equity loans, but I find that the "credit line" or "revolving credit line" is most useful. This type of loan allows me to write a check whenever I need it without having to get approval as long as I stay within my credit line. Purchasing a property with your own credit line will save you thousands of dollars in points, attorney review fees, and other closing costs as well.

Seller financing is another possibility that can help you to get around the 20% down amount. More and more, sellers are holding mortgages, or at least part of a mortgage to help sell their properties. This is a good way to break into the rental business. The seller benefits because he is able to sell a property he may be having difficulty selling. Also, he will have a steady income from the sale and interest on the property. Depending on age and position, this could be a wonderful supplement to retirement income, and if the property was an investment for them, they could benefit by not having to pay all of the capital gains tax on the sale of the property in a lump sum. Although this type of financing is on the increase, it still represents a small percentage of the total sales. You are fortunate to find such a deal. You won't know until you ask. We will discuss this type of purchase in a later chapter.

Finally, the partnership. This vehicle of investment has advantages as well as disadvantages. My first venture into real estate investment was a partnership. A total of five of us, all friends in this case, wanted to invest in a four-unit apartment. This would be the first in a series of purchases and sales that would make us all financially well off, or so we thought!

Expectations were high and enthusiasm abounded. Each put in an equal amount of seed money to set up a corporation, accounting, and down payment funds. We would borrow enough to purchase the property and make the necessary repairs. One definite advantage to the partnership is that the risk is spread around. Each of us invested $2,000 to start compared to a $10,000 investment for an individual.

As the settlement date approached we outlined a tentative schedule to begin the repairs and renovations. Shortly after settlement, reality set in. On the agreed day to begin, some were late, and some could not make it to the property for the workday. This would be a scene that would be repeated throughout the renovation period. There would be times when the 'friendship' became strained because most of the work was done by a few and not all in the group. In an ideal situation, an advantage of the partnership is the even distribution of the work that needs to be completed. If you are unfortunate enough to enter into a partnership where all members do not contribute their fair share, relations will be strained and friendships could dissolve.

Many times when financial decisions had to be made, we were not able to come to a consensus on exactly how something should be handled, or whether to go 'first class' 'second class', or 'no class' on a particular renovation or replacement part. The ideal situation is to give one or two members the authority to make such decisions. When the units were rented and tenant questions, problems, or needs arose, who was the lucky one to field the call? That honor usually fell to one or two individuals. Yours truly was one of the lucky ones to have calls at night concerning the heater or plumbing.

When the all of units were finally finished six months later, I had had enough of the unequally yoked partnership. We decided to sell the property and were successful a few months later. In all, we owned the property for about 13 months, and made a profit of $35,000. Thirty-five thousand dollars you say! Wow that's great for a one-year investment! On the surface, this is a wonderful profit considering the purchase price was $60,000. However, once the money was divided equally, each share was $4,000 in profit. Let's pay the attorney, accountant, and state and federal governments their share of taxes, and the real net profit dwindled to about $3,000 each--for six months work. The real estate agent who sold the house earned $6,000 in commission for only several hours of work. I made $3,000 for countless hours of sweat and aggravation.

That moment, a light bulb popped on, or maybe it was a sledge hammer that hit me. Perhaps it would be a good idea to earn my real estate license. It certainly seemed like a good way to earn money. A few years later I did get my license, and it has aided me in finding investment properties, and knowing more about the market in my area.

Anyway, the property was sold, and I had a decision to make. Would I continue in the partnership, strike out on my own, or quit the real estate game altogether? I certainly felt the concept of being a landlord or real estate investor was a worthy one. I felt that real estate could be a means of support, especially for the long term, and possibly for the short term as well. I did not want to give up the idea, but I knew that I did not want to continue in the partnership.

What looked like a great idea on paper did not play out the way some of us expected. However, with the right chemistry, proper identification of roles and duties, the partnership could be a very useful mechanism for acquiring properties and accumulating an impressive real estate portfolio. It may work well with 'silent partners', ones who perhaps would put up the investment capital, while others would do the actual work. A formula for the profit

distribution could be worked out, and all members would be satisfied in their

own capacity. Any partnership should work and could work if all parties

understand and then adhere to their particular responsibilities.

CHAPTER 4

FINDING PROPERTIES

Once you've decided to take the plunge, the next step is to find a property that will have the potential to generate the profits that fit your goals. There are several places to begin your search which include local realtors, the internet, newspapers, individuals, HUD properties, tax sales, sheriff's sales, and bank foreclosures.

THE REALTOR

Your local realtor may be the best source when starting. The reason is that he or she has access to many properties at once through the Multiple Listing Service. You can go to the realtor's office, sit down at the computer and find several properties that fit the description of the property that you are interested in. Properties are listed by area and by price, so it will be easy to pinpoint what is available at any particular time. The listings are updated each day, so have your realtor check daily for any properties that you might be interested in.

If you can find a real estate agent who will truly take your best interest to heart, he or she will be on "the lookout" and notify you as soon as properties that fit your specifications come onto the market. Ask the agent how many investors he is working with, and if he is in the investment business himself. Ask this because if he is purchasing properties for investment purposes, he will get first shot at properties before he notifies you. When I first began to look for properties, I made known my intentions to several local agents and never once received a call about an investment property. Only later did I realize that these agents were investors themselves, and I wasn't going to be able to move in on their territory. A good agent will stick with you for the duration. You might not purchase the first property that he brings to your attention, or the second, or the tenth. It is hoped that he will have the insight that you will become a repeat customer once you get your business established.

THE INTERNET

The Internet has become a vast resource for anyone searching for a home or an investment properties. Almost instantaneously one can have a significant amount of information on any property for sale in a given area and price range.

As a realtor, I search my local multiple listing daily for any new listing that becomes available. When a client asks me to help locate investment properties, initially I send a complete list of available properties in the price range and areas desired. Then, as new properties become available, I immediately send, via email, the listing information to my buyer.

As an investor, you should secure the services of a local realtor to help you in this manner. In my area we don't have buyers sign any type of agreement that will bind them to us as customers. Find an agent you are comfortable working with, and if for some reason they don't provide the service you require, kindly tell them so, and move on to another agent. It is in your best interest to be working with one agent, not multiple ones. As an agent, if I know that you are working with multiple agents---to be perfectly honest---I might not be inclined to work as hard for you as I would a client who uses me exclusively. You will earn the same level of loyalty as you give!

Beyond my local multiple listing, one can find properties on many sites including, but not limited to, Realtor.com, Century21.com (which is the company that I work for) and many other ".com's" including Move, Google, Trulia, Yahoo, Openhouse, Zillow, MSN, and Cyberhomes. Most of your local agencies have their own sites as well.

If, while searching the various sites, you see a property for which you want additional information, note the address, MLS (multiple listing) number, agent and phone, and call your agent. He or she will secure the additional information and schedule an appointment if so desired.

Some of the above mentioned sites display more information than others. Some are not as accurate or up to date.

NEWSPAPERS

Newspapers, specifically the classified ads and sometimes small display ads, and real estate publications, offer another valuable source for the potential investor. Most of the time, these advertisements are placed by real estate offices and agents, but more and more, we can find individuals who are selling their properties without the help of a real estate office. I will expand on sales by owner shortly. In my area, local agents collectively advertise in real estate magazines that are placed as inserts in local papers or placed in common areas such as grocery stores, professional offices, churches etc. for the public to have easy access. Pictures and a short description of the properties and sometimes the price and exact location are included. Sometimes there is only the description and picture so that you will need to call the real estate office to get further information and give a particular agent the opportunity to show you the property. Advertising is very expensive, so the realtor will not be advertising all of the properties at any one time.

INDIVIDUAL SELLERS

More and more frequently, we see properties that are being sold by individuals without the help of real estate offices. These properties are referred to as 'for sale by owner', or FSBO'S. I suppose the main reason for an individual to sell his own property is to avoid paying the sales commission to the agent, normally 6% of the selling price. The beginner may find it difficult and frustrating to attempt to market his own property. The owner must pay for the yard sign and all advertising of the property. He or she must also make the appointments to show the property, and if a buyer is found, possibly help the buyer to secure financing. Then there is the matter of ordering the title work, survey, preparing the contract and Deed, among other things.

One disadvantage to selling a property on your own is the amount of exposure that you will receive. Unless you are prepared to spend a good deal on advertising, the only prospective buyers that you will contact are the ones who actually drive by the property and see the sign in the yard.

However, being on the purchasing side, you, as an investor, may reap some benefits from the sale by owner. One such benefit may be a lower selling price since the seller does not have to pay a commission. He may be willing to take a lower amount for the property because he does not have the cost of the commission built into the asking price. Another benefit might be that the owner is in a position to either hold the entire mortgage on his own or hold part of the mortgage. This option could conceivably save you thousands of dollars in closing costs and could drastically reduce the amount of out of pocket money you will need to purchase this property. If you do find an individual who is willing to hold some or all of the mortgage, be prepared to pay a slightly higher interest rate. This is not always the case, but usually the owner financing will see higher rates. This is not necessarily bad for you, the investor. Once you own the property, should the mortgage rates fall significantly, you always have the option to refinance. Owner financing can work to your benefit.

HUD PROPERTIES

A HUD property is one that is owned by the division of Housing and Urban Development of the Federal Government. The properties are those whose previous owners have defaulted on their mortgages. These mortgages were backed by the government. When owners defaulted, the government paid off the balance and took over the property. The government then attempts to re-sell the property on the open market. Recently, these properties are listed with some local agency in each particular area.

These homes are usually an excellent opportunity for the investor. Often these homes have been vacant for months or longer and are in need of repair. Sometimes the repairs are quite extensive. Usually the property is boarded up with a HUD sign in the window with a federal case number and telephone number. You must use a real estate agent to purchase these homes. The agency sign is usually on the home as well.

If you see such a property, contact your real estate agent to gain access. If you've made known your desire to look at HUD properties to your agent, he will call you each week that there is a property that fits the particular parameters of your desired property. The agent will have the key for these properties and will be happy to show you through.

Now, when inspecting these properties, be prepared. They are usually boarded up, so take a flashlight. The electric and other utilities are not on. If, after viewing the property, it is something that you are interested in, you can have the utilities turned on, but you have certain procedures to follow. It is not easy to do this in the very short time that you have to make a bid on these properties. For the few HUD properties that I have purchased, I have not had the utilities turned on. When I go into one of these ventures, I know full well to expect the worst, while hoping for the best.

You purchase these properties strictly in an "as is" condition. HUD will supply no certifications--none. You assume the condition. Certifications such as plumbing, electric, heating, well and septic may be required by your bank. Check this out BEFORE you place your bid if possible. If you know that your lending institution will require these, you will need to begin to obtain the certifications as soon as you receive word that your bid is accepted.

If you choose to have the property "checked out", you may do so at your expense. It will need to be done in a timely manner so that you still have time to submit your bid. Remember, to have most things checked, the utilities must be turned on first. Expect that things such as the hot water heater, heater, and maybe even the water and sewer lines, if the house is very old, will probably need to be replaced. Be prepared.

Some HUD homes are for sale to owner/occupants only. This means that you must intend to use this property as your principal residence. Properties will be listed as either owner/occupants or for the general public. If you are an investor, you cannot purchase a property designated for owner/occupant.

The federal government wants to sell most of the properties to those who will use them as their principal home, which will help to stabilize neighborhoods and communities. Investors many times are seen as individuals who just want to make a quick buck, not caring much about the neighborhood. Investors might not maintain a property as well as the homeowner, only being concerned about receiving rent and not caring who moves into the property. While I agree in principle with this assessment, often times the property in question is in need of such extensive repairs, that the average prospective homeowner might not have the funds, time, or desire to renovate such a property. An investor often has the resources, whether it be time and/or capital, to renovate and prepare for re-sale, thus achieving the same goal that the government had in the first place. However, there are investors who purchase a property, do the absolute least amount of patch up or cosmetics, then try to rent for top dollar. This type of operation, 'the Band-Aid approach', will only create ill effects over the long run.

HUD does have a very interesting program for the investor or owner occupant which helps tremendously in the acquisition of properties. The 203K program helps the home buyer to purchase and renovate a HUD home. The government will lend the buyer a large portion of the purchase price and renovation costs. Thus, a buyer can purchase and renovate a HUD home as an owner-occupant or investor. Many local banks will handle the 203K, but some institutions specialize in this program. Ask around in your area to know ahead of time which lending institutions will be best equipped to help you.

In a nutshell, the 203K program works like this. Once your bid is approved, you sit down with your mortgage officer, and standard mortgage application process begins. The main differences will be that you are required to put down less than a conventional loan. You can get money for the purchase price of the property in the condition that it is now in. Then, you list the improvements that you think you will be making with an estimated cost for such improvements. An inspector will come to the property, review the improvements you listed, check the estimates you quoted, and then add any other improvements the FHA may require along with the estimated amount for these additional improvements. All costs for the improvements are totaled, and if approved, FHA will lend you, the buyer, approximately a percentage of the total costs. This amount is lumped together with the purchase price, into one amount which will be your mortgage amount.

The money for improvements will be released as draws over a certain period of time as the repairs are completed. You most likely will have the option to have the money divided into two, three, four, or more segments. As you complete renovations, you call for an inspection of the completed work, and once inspected, a portion of the money is released to you. This is not dissimilar to a construction loan where the bank releases money to the builder as portions of the project are completed. The 203K program is an excellent way to acquire HUD homes.

SHORT SALES

Since the recession of 2008, short sales have become more and more common. Homes are being sold for less that the owner owes on the property. A huge difference between the current asking price and the amount owed is not uncommon. The short sale is an excellent opportunity for a homeowner or investor. However, a word of caution, there are very few things " short" about a short sale. This process can take many months to complete. I have encountered banks that take three to four months just to get back to me on the initial offer. Contracts and a preliminary settlement sheet are prepared, then sent off to the participating bank. They get back to you when they are ready.

Most of the time, the buyer will be responsible for all costs concerning the closing, and will be buying the property " as-is". There are times however, where I have seen the bank spring for some of these costs. Each deal is different. For a few years, the banks did not want to budge on price, but now, finally in 2011 and 2012, it seems they are trying to streamline things. It makes no sense to drag things on as it costs money each day that the property sits—many times vacant—leaving the property prey to vandals and deterioration.

THE TAX SALE

A property goes up for tax sale when the owner becomes delinquent in his taxes for a long period of time, perhaps a year or eighteen months. The property can be "purchased" for the amount of taxes that are owed against the property. However, the purchaser cannot take possession of the property until two years after the tax sale, and then only if the amount of tax and interest has not been paid to you by the owner. The owner has two years to pay you back plus interest. If he does this, he retains the property, and you have your investment returned with interest. When a property is placed in a tax sale, potential investors bid to acquire the property. For example, if I own a property that is delinquent $3,000 in taxes, the city will publish my name, address, and the amount due. At a scheduled time, all those interested in bidding on my property gather together. The bidding is done with respect to the amount of interest that investors are willing to accept. To "purchase" my property, the investor must pay the city the original $3,000, then tell what interest rate he will accept. The rate may start as high as 18%. If no one else bids, the investor agrees to pay the $ 3,000 and accept a return of 18% on his investment. If I do not pay back this amount plus the interest, the investor will take possession of my property in two years. I can pay this amount back at any time within the two years and maintain possession of my property.

If, however, there are two or more bidders for my property, the one who accepts the lower interest rate will be the one who is awarded the winning bid. The tax sale is a good investment for the reason that your money is guaranteed and you are given a lien on the property. It is not likely that you can receive a greater return on your money in the bank. Also, there is that small possibility that you could actually take possession should the owner choose not to pay you.

BANK FORECLOSURES

If the mortgage on a property was one that was not backed by the federal government, the bank or lending institution will be forced to 'take back' the property in a situation where the owner defaults on the loan. The bank will attempt to re-sell or unload the property as soon as possible. The longer they delay, the more a property will cost the bank.

If you know or get to know bank representatives who deal with foreclosures, they may be willing to let you know about these properties in advance. All banks are different, but perhaps, they would be willing to give you a mortgage on the property if you were to take it off their hands. This would eliminate costly delays for the bank. They then are able to turn a bad situation into one that becomes profitable.

There are also individuals who serve as "brokers" between owners who are about to be foreclosed upon and potential investors. They earn their money in the form of a fee that is assessed to the seller. They hopefully can take a situation where an owner is about to lose his home and salvage something for the owner as well as find an investor who is happy to assume the balance owed, an amount that will allow him to turn a profit either in the long term or the short term.

I know of another group that will approach owners who are about to lose their homes. They make a deal that allows the investor to take title to the property, rent it back to the owner while any renovations are made, then put the property up for sale and split the profit with the owner. This allows the owner to retain some of the equity that he has accumulated in the property, gives the owner a place to live for the renovation period, and perhaps keep some of the profit that is earned through the sale of the house.

BUILDING INSPECTORS

The local building inspector may be able to point you to some properties that are available. Inspectors may know of properties that have code violations, and for whatever reason, the owners may not want to correct the violations. It's possible that these properties could be purchased for a very reasonable amount. Usually, if the property has attracted the attention of the building inspector, there will be work to do on the property, sometimes considerable work.

Perhaps the property is owned by someone who wants or needs to get rid of the property immediately and can't afford to make the necessary repairs.

People you talk to who have some involvement or association with building, property, or investments increase the chances you have of locating possible income properties for yourself, even before the properties go on the market.

CHAPTER 5

CHOOSING THAT "GEM" OF AN INVESTMENT

Here's where we get into the "nitty gritty". So roll up your sleeves, sharpen that pencil, and get out the calculator. It has been said that beauty is in the eye of the beholder. What is beauty, or a gem to one person, may not be beauty or a gem to another. It has also been said that the three most important rules and guidelines for purchasing real estate are 1) Location, 2) Location, and 3) Location. I do not dispute that, but I have strayed from the rule on occasion. The beginning investor must make decisions based on his or her goals and financial situation at the time of investing.

Real estate, specifically income-producing property, has at least three ways to earn you money and help you achieve your financial goals, be it for the short term or long term.

Cash flow is the term that relates to the amount of money that comes in to you (rents) versus the amount of money that you must put out to maintain the property (mortgage principal and interest, taxes, insurance, utilities, repairs, supplies, advertising, etc.). You have a positive cash flow if your rents are greater than the amount of money that you put out each month. In a typical situation, some months will have a greater cash flow than others simply because taxes and utilities are billed quarterly instead of monthly. Some months you will have repairs, while other months you will not. I usually determine the cash flow over the course of a year (adding the rents for the year and subtracting the expenses for the year, and then dividing by twelve) to get an accurate picture of the cash flow. Hopefully you will take in more than you put out.

Equity gain is what I call a hidden benefit. This is the amount that you pay in principal each month in your mortgage payment. Depending on the amount of your mortgage, interest rate, term (how many years), and how long you've had the mortgage, your amount of equity gain each month will vary. Shorter term and lower rates will boost the amount that your equity is increased each month. Whenever possible, I try to get the shorter term (15 years versus 20 or 30 years) in order to pay off the loan faster. Sometimes this might not be feasible because of the cash flow. The longer term mortgage will increase your cash flow each month, but will take longer to pay off the mortgage, thus costing you more money in interest in the long run. In a following chapter on amortization, you will be able to see actual examples of loans with different rates and terms, and how the payments and total interest vary.

I view the properties that I purchased as a savings investment. Even though we don't see the equity gain as a tangible 'in your pocket' benefit, over the course of the mortgage, the property will be paid for. We don't literally "touch" the gain, but know that it is accumulating. When I sell the property, I will realize that gain. If I purchase a property for $60,000, I know that at the end of the fifteen years that property will be paid for, and in a sense, I have saved, or accumulated $60,000 that I will get when I sell the property. If your goal were to accumulate ten such properties, even if your cash flow were zero, you would still have accumulated $600,000 in equity gain, not to mention appreciation.

Appreciation is another way that your real estate holdings will earn money over the time that you hold property. If you purchased a property now for $70,000, the hopes and expectations are that over time that property will increase in value. If the property increases just one percent per year, over ten years that property increases ten percent or approximately $7,000. Your property is now worth $77,000. The market or climate of real estate is a determining factor in appreciation. This climate is influenced by supply, demand, interest rates, and location. Properties generally appreciate more in better locations. This is a definite advantage to buying properties in more desirable neighborhoods.

In the early eighties, then again in the early 2000's, the selling prices soared. It was a good time to be selling your home or investment property. Since then, some areas have actually seen a loss in value of property for different reasons. Owners in some cases now owe more on their mortgage than the property is worth. So appreciation is not always guaranteed over the short term. Research the property, the neighborhood, and the community before purchasing in order to get as accurate a value and chance of appreciation as possible.

So, where is your "gem"? The answer to that question is wherever you fit in financially and wherever you feel comfortable. The better locations will provide, in many cases, better maintained properties. Newer homes should mean less maintenance. Nicer neighborhoods should result in more desirable tenants, tenants who may be professionals and middle or upper- middle class economically. Rents normally will be higher. Appreciation should be better, thus increasing the value of your investment. Properties in better locations are generally easier to re-sell.

A drawback for the beginning investor for these properties will be the start up costs and a cash flow that may be small or non-existent. Nicer properties cost more money. Taxes are higher. You will need a bigger down payment and will have a larger mortgage. If you are in a position financially to ride out the long term with little or no cash flow and bank on appreciation, properties in better neighborhoods at higher prices might be the way to go.

The beginner, as was my case, doesn't always have the luxury of big down payments. I needed to have a positive cash flow to cover any problem that might occur, including the possibility of a vacant unit for a month or longer. Rent lost because a unit is not occupied can never be recovered. It is essential to keep vacancies at a minimum. Empty units have a negative effect on your budget and financial goals.

You need to find the area that you are most comfortable with. We would all like to have higher scale properties that bring in lots of rent with a great cash flow and no maintenance problems. Creative deals make this scenario more of a possibility, but, to this point, I have gotten away from that thinking and have purchased properties that were in older neighborhoods, needing some or extensive work. I have purchased properties in order to make rentals out of them full knowing that appreciation will be small. I purchase properties I feel that I can rent and have good positive cash flow. These properties are older and will require more maintenance, but the cash flow will cover these expenses. My goal is to have the property pay for itself over a fifteen year period. I assume that I will be able to get at least what I paid for the property when I go to sell fifteen years later. If appreciation occurs, so much the better. If not, the worst that has happened is that I have accumulated "x" number of dollars in equity.

Now, older properties usually sell for less, thus requiring a smaller amount of start-up capital, but be prepared for some expenses to renovate and maintain. In the pages that follow, I will give several examples of properties that I have purchased along with the necessary costs, fixed expenses, and cash flow. We will also review examples of higher priced properties, and the costs associated with them.

As far as cash flow goes, I try to choose properties that will yield at least $100 to $150 per unit per month. At times I have been fortunate to receive more, depending on the given situation. Some landlords are happy to break even, banking on appreciation and equity gain. Obviously, the more the better. Be patient in your search. Sooner or later you will find properties that yield the desired cash flow.

The first property that I purchased on my own was a three-unit property. The main building had two units, and there was also a detached cottage. It was in a rural area and the asking price was $35,000. I knew that it needed work. I was hoping that $10,000 would be the maximum for repairs and renovations. I did very little checking into the units to get an accurate determination of the extent of repairs. I later found that to be an expensive lesson because I ended up spending more than twice what I hoped in order to have all the units ready. ALWAYS check out a property as much as possible. Watch out for the "majors"-the majors being heat, roof, electric, plumbing, well and septic/ water and sewer.

If you are buying a property through a realtor, and the realtor knows of a problem, he is obligated to tell you of the problem. The owner of the property must disclose known problems as well. There are different ways to have a property checked out. There are individuals/companies who are professional inspectors. For a fee (usually $250-$400), these inspectors will make a detailed assessment of any problem areas of the property that you are interested in. Usually they will earn their keep, finding trouble areas that, if the seller corrects, will save you money in the long run.

If you decide not to use these home inspectors, you must rely on your knowledge, and perhaps the knowledge of your friendly plumber, electrician, etc. If you do not know one of these individuals personally who might do an inspection as a friend, you will have to pay each inspector separately.

If you decide to rely strictly on your knowledge and inspection and you are not well versed in the 'trades', there are a few things that you can specifically look for. Areas that are cause for major expense should they need replacing are the roof, heating, plumbing, water/sewer or well/septic, and electric.

The roof can be inspected form the outside for deterioration of the shingles and the adjoining wood (soffit and fascia). If the shingles are brittle or cracked, it is a good bet that they will have to be replaced in the near future. Buckling, rolling shingles are not a good sign. From the attic, you can tell what kind of material is under the shingles. If you have a plywood roof, that's good news because a new roof will entail taking off only the old shingles and replacing them with new ones. Some older roofs have a wood base called tongue and groove. This is not as easy to work with as plywood, but does not have to be replaced while changing the shingles. Older homes have cedar shakes as their base. When this type of roof is replaced, all of the shakes must come off and be replaced with plywood. This will increase the cost of a new roof substantially.

The heating system can also be costly to replace. It is wise to have included in your contract-to-purchase a clause stating that the heating and plumbing is in good working order. If this is not possible, have the system checked out. Gas-fired hot air seems to be the ever growing popular choice. Oil furnaces tend to have more service problems, especially with tenants who allow the oil to run too low in the tank, or tenants who choose the cheapest oil they can find which sometimes is not the best grade. Oil tanks could be the cause of problems over the years as well. I am not saying to avoid properties with oil heaters, just be aware of potential problems. Gas furnaces are usually more expensive to replace. Personally, I stay away from homes that are heated by electric. Since the tenant will be responsible for the electric, the heating costs obviously become his concern, but a home heated by electric is less attractive to the tenant because of the high cost. Also, when it is time to sell, you will find that a property with electric heat will have a more difficult time selling. However, with soaring oil and gas prices, the electric heating may be a little more attractive. Again, another individual decision to be based on the costs in one's particular area.

Other things related to the heating system are duct work or baseboard, whichever is the case. Check for rusted duct work or broken, rusty, damaged or missing baseboard in each room. Inspect the oil tank for rust (especially on the bottom). Is it outside, or in the basement? If the tank is outside, it will be easier to replace if there is a problem, but the line must be protected against freezing. A tank that is inside will usually have to be cut out to be removed, thus adding to the cost and potential mess. If underground, you may be subject to present or future regulation from the EPA (Environmental Protection Agency). The tank may have to be tested and possibly removed in the very near future. It is becoming more and more likely that insurance companies will not insure properties that have underground tanks.

Concerning the plumbing, it is important to determine the type of pipes that supply the water, whether or not the sinks and fixtures are trapped properly, are there any leaks under the sinks or around the tub or toilet fixture, and what the water pressure is.

Older homes might still have the galvanized piping. If the piping hasn't already been changed to copper or plastic, the chances are good that you will have to replace the piping in the near future. Always do a walk-through inspection the day of or day before closing to double check the plumbing and other areas of concern.

Check under the sinks for proper plumbing (traps, etc.) and look for any rotted wood under the pipes, or pots and pans to catch dripping water. Run the faucets, and while they are on, flush the toilet. This will give you some indication of the water pressure. Do the faucets leak when they are turned on? Are they corroded or rusty?

City or public water and sewer is my preference over well and septic systems. Each has advantages and disadvantages. The city water and sewer lines, if in good condition seem to have fewer service problems. However, a city line that has roots, or collapses, or runs under sidewalks and driveways, can be a real challenge to repair. Old water lines have a tendency to need replacement over time as well. You will pay a fee, usually quarterly, to the municipality for the water that you use, as well as a sewer charge. Presently, in my town the cost is $85 per quarter for the sewer, and $25 per quarter (minimum, and does go higher depending on usage) for the water. These costs are PER UNIT. So a rental with two units will pay each fee twice per quarter.

With well and septic systems, one does not have these quarterly costs. However, should you have a problem with either, the cost of repair or replacement can be substantial. My first property had a well and septic system. The property had three units working off one well and septic system, and although the septic system had to be pumped more often, it cost less than having to pay for three units each quarter. Fortunately, I did not have any major problems with the well nor the septic system during the time that I owned the property.

Some aspects of the electric can be readily inspected by simply finding the panel box, usually in the basement. If the property still has fuses, it is advisable to have a new service installed. Also, inspect as many areas as possible for evidence of old wiring. The most common areas of exposed wiring will be in the basement, crawl spaces, and the open attic. Older wiring should be replaced, and may result in your having a difficult time finding homeowners insurance to protect your investment.

Termite and/or structural damage can be the most expensive to repair. If you suspect such structural damage, you should hire an engineer to give you an expert opinion. As far as termite damage, it might be worth your time, effort, and cost to have a qualified pest control agency to inspect the property even before you make the purchase. The seller will have to provide a termite certification to the buyer at the time of closing. The cost of the certification may be the responsibility of the buyer if negotiated as such in the contract. If you are purchasing a HUD home, it is solely the buyer's responsibility. HUD supplies no certifications.

When inspecting a property, I try to determine the potential the property has as a rental as well as re-sale down the road. I look for space to use as an additional half bath, or possibly even another bedroom. Many older houses were 'chopped up' or added onto in such a way that would lend itself to restructuring some areas for more useful space.

The extra half a bath will be worth the time and money to add if possible. The re sale value will more than compensate for the cost. Also, the more bedrooms a property has the better the possibility of higher rents as well as added value upon selling.

The number of bedrooms, bathrooms, as well as the layout and modernization of the kitchen area, are extremely important in the marketability of a property whether for re-sale or as a rental.

CHAPTIER 6

WHEN YOU OWN YOUR INVESTMENT PROPERTY

Before buying your property, you should have decided whether to use it as a rental property for the long term, or as a property to renovate if needed, then 'flip'. By flip, I mean to turn over for resale as soon as you have completed any necessary renovations. This type of short term venture can be rewarding as well. I will discuss this in greater detail in another chapter. If you haven't decided by the time your purchase is complete, don't fret. It's just that I have a good idea what my plans are before starting a particular project. Depending on those plans, the amount of renovation (big time or cosmetic) and the quality of new items (carpet, range, cabinets, etc.) will vary.

I never buy the cheapest materials. If the property is a property that I plan to keep as a rental, it is very likely that cheap things will wear out, break, and ultimately have to be replaced sooner or later---usually sooner. For a rental, I don't necessarily buy the best of materials either because of the potential use and or abuse that materials will be subject to. In my first few rental properties, I placed a good quality sculptured carpet throughout. I made the apartment look as though I myself would be living there. For some strange reason, the same carpet that lasted many years in my own home was lasting two or three years in the rental property. The good carpet and padding just wasn't working out for the rentals. Since then, I use a commercial grade of carpet in almost every case for the rental property. It still looks nice, and it wears much longer. You have a wide variety of colors to choose from. It is easier to replace and costs significantly less. I usually choose a neutral color (a middle shade of brown for the living room, dining room, stairs and hall which are the highest traffic areas. I might get creative with the bedrooms, choosing a different color for each room. Some of my friends who are landlords just pick one neutral color and carpet the entire unit with that particular color.

Paint for the rental properties should be a semi-gloss or eggshell rather than flat. Although the flat is cheaper, it tends to show all kinds of marks and does not clean up very well. Many times with the semi-gloss and eggshell, marks wipe off, and the finish seems to last longer. I don't get too creative with colors. I usually paint most of the rooms off-white, and the kitchen and bathroom white. Sometimes I do paint the baseboard and woodwork a white, and sometimes it is the same color as the room. The fewer colors you have to deal with the better. It is easier and less time consuming. Many landlords whom I know use the same color for all of the rooms and all of the units.

This allows you to purchase larger quantities of paint at a lower price per gallon and makes touch ups easier to match. Also, it may eliminate having to paint an entire room over instead of just the soiled areas.

In a rental, if I have the choice between a $500 starter kitchen set (sink and basic cabinets) or $1200 unit, I will choose the starter kitchen. Cheap faucets will always come back to haunt you. Better to get a good unit with parts that you know can be replaced in the future than choosing a fly-by-night model for half the price or less. Sooner or later you will end up buying the more expensive faucet.

I try to be more economical with rentals without being 'cheap'. I never Band-Aid a problem because if I do, that same problem will re-occur within a short time. Take care of the problem the first time. It may cost a little more initially, but it will be well worth it in the long run.

When working on a property for resale, I try to use the best materials within reason. The cost of the property and potential re sale value will determine how much you can spend and still make an acceptable profit. Cabinets, carpet, updates such as plumbing, heating, electrical, tile, are all things that you can do to increase your profit and chances of selling. Other features such as screened porches, half-baths, fencing, and landscaping are great if they fit into your budget for this type of investment property.

Windows and doors seem to take a beating in rental units that house several children. I don't know how many times I have replaced screens and even glass that broke because of abuse. In one particular property that had a nice storm door and wooden outside door, I had to replace the screen three times and repair the frame twice. Even though the tenant is responsible for these repairs, it is still a headache that is time consuming, one that you can do without. Finally, after checking with the city inspectors, I ended up putting in a steel door. That put an end to those repair problems.

In my neck of the woods, the landlord always supplies the range, and a refrigerator is optional. Very rarely have I supplied the refrigerator. In my very first rental property, I supplied three new ranges and three new refrigerators. You might ask, why new? Well at the time I thought that was the thing to do. However, it doesn't have to be that way. I have found over the years and through experience with both new and used, if I am going to be responsible for the appliance, then I would rather have a new one that is not likely to have service problems. The times that I put a used appliance in a unit, inevitably there were service problems. Even if it is a simple problem, the cost of the service call and then the repair cost can be considerable. If you end up with a serious or expensive problem, often times it is better to replace the unit instead of repairing. This is true especially with the range.

On a few occasions, the property that I purchased came with a refrigerator. In that case I would tell the tenant that he was welcome to use it, but it was his responsibility to maintain it. If he wanted his own, then that was up to him. A few times, the tenant who was to move into the unit did not have a refrigerator and did not have the funds to purchase a new one. I offered to purchase the new one but the rent would increase by say $20 or $25. He was happy, and I had increased the rent enough to cover the cost in about 2 years. I would not recommend this on a regular basis, but if I find a good tenant, then I will do whatever I can within reason to help the process along.

CHAPTER 7

WILL YOUR PROPERTY MAKE MONEY

How will you know if you have a property that will make money? Let's first define "making money". As mentioned earlier, your property can make money in three different ways: positive cash flow, equity gain, appreciation. As a landlord, you need to define making money in your terms. Ask yourself, "Do I need a positive cash flow, or am I satisfied by simply breaking even and settling for the gain from equity as I make my monthly mortgage payments? Some landlords are happy just "breaking even." You may find that you have to settle for this depending on the property that you choose. Some landlords will not purchase a property unless they can realize a predetermined amount of positive cash flow, say, $100, $150 or more per month per unit.

You might ask, how can anyone settle for just breaking even? Good question. One of the benefits to owning investment property is the depreciation factor which will reduce the amount of taxes that the owner has to pay. This reduction is a benefit that helps ease the pain of little or no cash flow. We will talk more about depreciation in a future chapter.

A good rule of thumb is to try to have a cash flow of $150 and up per month per unit. When things go well, this positive flow will add up to a substantial amount at the end of the year. However, things, as you might guess, don't always go well. The unit will from time to time need maintenance and repair. Hopefully the repairs will be minor (new faucet, new outlet, etc). Sometimes, though, a major repair will come your way. Hot water heaters, paint jobs, new roof, and others will find you out sooner or later. The positive cash flow, if at all possible, should be set aside for such rainy days. The repairs and maintenance are deductible expenses, but they still have to be paid for.

If you find that you have accumulated a tremendous amount from your positive cash flow, then let your imagination suggest fun-filled ways to spend it. In addition to buying something for myself for all of the hard work and stressful situations that I have encountered in my rental business, I like to apply as much money as I can to the principal amount of my mortgage. This allows me to have the property paid for sooner, thus saving me interest.

One other expense that might not be so obvious is the empty apartment expense. When banks calculate the value of your property before you purchase it, one of the ways they do it is through an income approach, approximating the rents that you will receive in a year. They also figure a 'vacancy rate' of approximately 5% of the total rents. For example, if your rent is $500 per month, when you multiply that by 12 months, the total rent for the year is $6,000. Five percent of $6,000 is $300, so they may figure that your total income for the year is $5,700 ($6,000 minus the $300 for vacancy). Vacancy is an absolute concern for the landlord. I have been very fortunate over the years to keep this loss at a minimum. Rent lost because of empty units can NEVER be made up. In most cases, I have been able to rent an empty unit within two weeks. There have been a few times that an apartment stayed empty for two or three months. At just $500 per month, that's a loss of $1,000 to $1,500 which will never be recovered.

So, how do we find out ahead of time how much money we are able to make on a particular unit? The first thing that I do is to try and determine how much rent I can receive on the unit in question. Do your homework. Check the classified section of your newspaper to see what other landlords are charging for their units. Compare other units with yours, noting what utilities are included, location, size, and additional features. Is your unit in a better location than another? Identical units can demand different rents depending on location. Some units include utilities. My advice concerning utilities would be, if at all possible, to hold the tenants responsible to pay the utilities. It's amazing how conservation-minded a tenant becomes when he is responsible for the heat. Certainly, there are conscientious tenants, but I had one who liked to open the windows when it was 20 degrees outside instead of turning the heat down.

Sometimes it is not possible to have the tenants pay the heat. If you have two or more units in a building which is serviced by only one heater, you will have to adjust your rent accordingly to have the heat included. In such a building, I would advise to have the utilities separated if possible. Initially this could be a hefty expense, but in the long run it will end up paying for itself. Also, having the utilities separated is a good selling feature if and when you decide to sell your property.

The amount of rent is also determined by the number of bedrooms in the unit. The more bedrooms, the higher the rent. In my area, there is quite a demand for three and four bedroom units. The demand is adequate for two bedrooms, and not so great for one bedroom. One reason for the low demand for one bedroom is that there are so many of them. The law of supply and demand works against me for a one bedroom apartment. One bedroom units are the hardest to rent, but they do have some advantages. First, your prospective tenants for a one bedroom unit might be a single, or a young couple just getting started, or perhaps a Senior Citizen couple or individual. In most of these cases, you have individuals who have no children. This will keep the wear and tear to a minimum. One disadvantage is the lower rent. Another is that singles tend to get married and need a bigger place. Couples tend to have children, which also requires a larger apartment. Both of these groups may be the cause for a turnover of the unit more frequently than you would like. This is generally speaking of course and is not always the case.

Three and four bedroom units are in great demand and will bring a higher rent. However, one reason for the need of the multi-bedroom unit is the size of the family. Again, generally speaking and not always the case, large families tend to produce more wear and tear requiring more maintenance of your unit.

These are all things that you need to consider when buying an investment property. You might decide to buy only one-bedroom units. Or maybe you are okay with multi-bedroom units. I have a combination and would suggest that you try the same.

Rents for a one bedroom apartment in my area range from $600 to $800 depending on the amount of utilities included, size, and location. Two-bedroom units range from $700 to $950, three-bedroom from $850 to $1100, and a four bedroom from $1000 to $1300 per month. Section 8 rents are slightly higher if you choose to rent to those on this rental assistance program. I will discuss in more detail the Section 8 program in a future chapter.

In your calculation, figure conservatively. For example, if your unit has two bedrooms in a decent location, figure the middle of the range. If in actuality you receive more, great. But for the sake of determining what cash flow you will receive, it is better to be on the safe side.

I would certainly advise that you check the rents for other apartments in your area. Check for the amount of rent as well as location to see how other units compare with yours. It is also a good idea for you to actually go and see other units so that you can make the best possible comparison. Let me say at this time that before you show your unit to prospective tenants, make sure that it is clean and ready to go. I can't tell you how many times people who have viewed my apartments commented on how clean the unit was. They then proceeded to tell me of other units they viewed, and how dirty some of them were. They couldn't believe, and neither could I, that other landlords would present their properties for rent in a dirty condition or a state of disrepair.

You might even consider posting your rent slightly lower than your competition as a way of attracting the better tenants to your units. If you are able to secure a good tenant because of the slightly lower rent, it will be worth the difference that you would have received.

Now, how much will your apartment cost to operate? There are several things to consider. First, and probably most costly, will be your mortgage payment. Your principal and interest amounts are determined by how much you are financing and the interest rate that you are paying. The monthly amount also depends on the length of your mortgage. Longer term means a smaller payment, but over the long haul you will end up paying more. See the chapter on amortization for some in-depth examples.

You will need to carry insurance on the property. You will want to carry enough fire insurance to cover the replacement cost of your unit. You will also want to carry a sufficient amount of liability insurance to protect you in the event of a claim due to injury on your property. These rates will vary from company to company and area to area.

Another cost for the unit is the water and sewer charge if you have public supplies. These charges are for each unit. For example, in my hometown, the quarterly charge for sewer is presently $85, and the minimum charge for water is $25 per quarter. If the amount of water used is over the basic minimum amount, the charge increases. As a landlord, I pay the sewer and minimum water each quarter. Any excess water bill is charged to the tenant. The water and sewer together total $110 per quarter, or, rounding off, about $40 per month.

The cost that you cannot determine in advance is the amount needed for repairs. This amount obviously will vary from month to month and year to year. I have had years where I had to spend almost nothing on repairs. Then there were times when a major expense hit me. A new hot water heater might cost $300 or more. Painting, new windows, faucets, or roof repair will sooner or later pay a visit to you. A service call for your heater will run you a minimum of $70 per hour if you are unfortunate enough to need the service in the evening. This is one reason to let your cash flow build up into a reserve. When problems come, your funds will be there to take care of them.

One hidden cost most of us tend to ignore or forget about is the amount of interest that we pay on the down payment money we use to buy the property. This cost is not figured in when I determine my cash flow for a property, but, nevertheless, it is a real expense. Suppose you withdrew $5,000 from your savings to put down on your property. Granted the interest that you were earning in a savings account may not be much, but it is interest that you will not be receiving now. Or if you cashed in some stock or mutual fund, the money that you would have earned is no longer coming in. So, in a sense this is a cost of operation to you.

Once you have figured the fixed costs, subtract them from the amount of rent that you expect to receive, and you will have the amount of positive cash flow each month. In the pages that follow I will present some examples of properties that I purchased, explaining the cash flow for each property. I will also give you a history of the property as far as rental information, purchase price, refinancing, etc. There are examples of a single home, duplex, triplex, and quad (four units). Follow along, work the numbers, and determine if these examples would be good investments for you. I learned the hard way on some of these, especially the first couple. I hope that you will learn from my mistakes, save yourself a lot of headaches, and keep more money in your pocket from having read these accounts.

Prices and expenses will vary from area to area, and by time period. However, the principles remain the same. You can work the numbers in the same fashion regardless of selling prices, etc.

SAMPLE PURCHASE #1
SINGLE FAMILY DWELLING
LISTING PRICE $65,000

Single family homes are desirable properties for investors.

Some advantages include:

Detached unit

More desirable for potential tenants

Higher re-sale value

Some of the disadvantages might include:

Higher cost per unit

Smaller positive cash flow

When vacant, owner may have to come up with funds to maintain

For the sake of example, let's say that we are financing the entire amount. This may not be the case, but remember, if you put money down from your savings, it is still costing you the interest that you would have received.

Note the following monthly expenses for this sample property.

	15 years	30 years
Principal and Interest on $65,000 @ 8%	$621.17	$476.95
Taxes ($1404 per year)	$117.00	$117.00
Insurance ($504 per year)	$42.00	$42.00
Water and Sewer charges ($120 per quarter)	$40.00	$40.00
Total fixed charges per month	$820.17	$675.95

Possible income from rents: **$900 to $1200 per month***

*This number will vary considerably depending on location, condition, size, etc. Check the market in your area to get a good sampling of the rents that are being charged. As you will see, a single unit in this price range will be a challenge financially, especially if it is one of your first investments.

Cash Flow (monthly) for 15 years: $100 to $300
Cash Flow for 30 years: $225 to $500

The monthly cash flow is higher with the 30- year note, but you are paying more in interest and less in principal.

Equity gain for a 15- year note: Starts at $187.84
Equity gain on a 30- year note: Starts at $43.62

The equity gain must also be considered as earned, thus your net gain for this property is the total of cash flow and equity gained per month, depending on the term of the mortgage.

One last reminder: Don't overlook the repair expense. Some months may require no maintenance, but in other months, the expense could be considerable.

SAMPLE   PURCHASE   # 2
DUPLEX (2 UNITS)
SELLING PRICE $48,000

(This is an actual property that I purchased shortly into my investment experience)

Selling Price $48,000

Cost for improvements $7,000

Down payment $8,000

Two- 2 bedroom units, each renting for $525

This property was located in an older neighborhood, which was reflected in the lower price.   I expected the appreciation to be minimal over the years, but I knew that this property would be easy to keep rented. I took out a 15-year mortgage at 7 ¾ %.

Fixed Costs:

Principal and Interest	$376.51
Insurance	$60.00
Water and Sewer (2 units)	$80.00
Taxes ($1800 per year)	$150.00

Total Fixed Costs:	$666.51
Rents Received:	$1050.00

Positive Cash Flow per month	$383.49
Equity gain per month started at	$118.00

Net Gain per month	$501.49

*Other costs

    Repairs

    Interest lost from savings for down payment:

        Approximated at $62/month

**This property was sold several years later for $56,000. Appreciation was very little, as I expected, but the cash flow and equity gain made the property a good investment over the years.

SAMPLE #3

TRIPLEX

SELLING PRICE $76,500

The buyer had to put down $14,500.

Rents were $325, $550, $595 for a total of $1470.

Utilities were all separate, so tenants paid for all utilities.

Insurance premium was $960 per year.

Taxes were $ 1850 per year.

First Mortgage was in the amount of $62,000 @ 9.5%.

Let's analyze this purchase to see if it was a good deal for the buyer. The fixed monthly costs were as follows:

	15 years	30 years
Principal and Interest	$647.42	$ 521.33
Insurance	$80.00	$80.00
Taxes	$154.00	$154.00
Total Fixed Monthly Costs	$881.42	$755.33
Positive Cash Flow	$588.58	$714.67

This would appear to be a good investment with a good cash flow, and, indeed, it has been a good money maker for the buyer. However, to get an absolutely clear picture of how your investment is producing, don't forget to consider the following: Repairs, money (interest) lost from savings for the down payment, depreciation, rent increases over the years, and equity gain.

1) Repairs. This cost will vary from year to year. In some years the total amount for repairs will be minimal, while in other years, it could be substantial. These costs lower positive cash flow.

2) Down payment. On this particular transaction, the down payment was $14,500. If we figure that this amount would be earning interest at the

rate of 5%, the monthly cost due to lost interest would be $60. This is a negative effect on the investment.

3) Depreciation. This property will be depreciated approximately $2780 per year. This "expense" will benefit the buyer by lessening the amount of taxes due each year, perhaps by as much as $900, which means a positive effect of $75 or more per month.

4) Rent increases. If each unit's rent was increased by only $50 over the first five or six years, this would mean that the rents would increase by $150 per month. This will have a positive effect on the cash flow as well.

5) Equity gain. I call this the hidden benefit because the buyer doesn't actually realize this benefit until the property is sold. On a 15-year mortgage, the gain starts out at $157 per month, and by the fifth year the gain is nearly $250 per month. Note that on a 30-year mortgage, the equity gain is only $30 per month to start, and after 5 years the gain is only $50 per month. It takes 26 years to reach the point where the equity gain is $250 per month.

In this particular case, they buyer has since refinanced at a lower rate which increases the equity gain that much faster. The tenants are actually paying for the property, and at the end of the 15th year, or the 30th year, even if your property did not appreciate at all, the buyer has the equivalent of $76,500 in the bank, or $76,500 in equity.

SAMPLE # 4
CURRENT LISTING FOUR UNIT DWELLING
ASKING PRICE $99,900

Four (4) one bedroom apartments

> Total rents $23,700 per year/ $1975 per month
>
> Taxes $3736 per year/ $ 312 per month
>
> Insurance $850 per year/ $ 71 per month
>
> Water and Sewer (public) $1760 per year/ $147 per month
>
> Down payment (20%) $20,000 Seller is willing to take back a second
>
> mortgage @ 10%, but only for 15 years
>
> Mortgage $79,900 @ 7.75%

Fixed Monthly Costs:	15years
Principal and Interest (1st mortgage)	$752.08
Principal and Interest (2cd mortgage)	$214.92
Taxes	$312.00
Insurance	$71.00
Water and Sewer	$147.00
Total fixed Monthly costs	$1497.00
Positive cash flow per month	$478.00

Negative points to consider:

1) Vacancy rate. A conservative figure is normally 5%, which would mean a loss of rent of $1185 per year or about $100 per month. Sometimes, I hope this is your case, there will be no vacancies.

2) One-bedroom units. Remember there are advantages as well as disadvantages with these units. One of the disadvantages in my area is the vast supply of one-bedroom units. This supply makes it more difficult to rent.

3) Repairs. There will almost always be an expense here. Find out as much as possible about the property before you make the purchase. Any costs that can be anticipated should be figured in.

Positive points to consider:

1) Rent increases. Even an increase of $10 per month translates into $40 per month total, or a $480 per year increase in cash flow.

2) Depreciation expense. In the short term this will work for your benefit. With a selling price of $99,900, the depreciation will be approximately $3600 per year. Depending on your tax bracket, this could amount to savings of up to $1200 per year, or $100 per month.

3) Equity gain. The "hidden benefit" will be $ 284 per month at the outset from the two mortgages, and after five years, the equity gain will be $ 430 per month. At the end of 15 years, the property is paid for. Pay as much extra principal as possible on the second mortgage to shorten the term and gain equity faster.

4) Appreciation. Depending on the location and the real estate market, your property will have increased in value over the years. For example, your unit that you purchase for $99,900 may be worth $120,000 or more at the end of 15 years, and since your property is paid for, it's just like money in the bank. Even if your property does not appreciate, you still have equity in the amount of $99,900, for very rarely does real estate decrease in value over a long period.

CHAPTER 8

GETTING MY FEET WET

As I mentioned earlier, my first venture was a partnership with a group of friends. This was mentioned in the introduction, so I will not say much more about that property except that it was a four-unit building and we had a positive cash flow of about $800 per month. This was great because it covered any emergencies, and if one of the units was vacant, we still had more than enough to cover our expenses. We ended up selling the property in one year for a gross profit of $40,000. Partnerships can be a profitable way of accumulating and maintaining income properties. Responsibilities and expectations need to be clearly understood from the outset. Only then will you have an operation that runs smoothly.

The first property that I purchased on my own was a three-unit property. This was located in a neighboring town about twenty minutes from my home. The potential cash flow was very inviting, but I truly 'went to school' on this one. The partnership property mentioned above did not need many major repairs. This property did. Fatal mistake number one was my failure to have the property checked by people who knew what they were talking about. I agreed to purchase the property strictly "as is". I figured repairs would be under $5,000 total for all three units.

WRONG! One heating system had to be replaced, and when the inspector came in, he "red-flagged" the other system and chimney. Red flagged means that you can't use what you have and need to replace the existing system.

Fatal flaw number two: I hired a family member of a friend who said he knew what he was doing when he really did not. Whenever possible, get references from the contractors that can be checked. Also, get at least two and probably three estimates. Different contractors may have different ways of approaching the repair or new work. Listen to what each has to say and recommends. This friend of the family took me for a ride. He took forever to do the work, and chose the most expensive and most difficult-to-maintain systems. The estimate that he originally gave me was only one-third of what I actually spent to have the systems up, and then hundreds and maybe thousands of dollars more to maintain and have corrected in the next several years.

The wiring in the house was a nightmare. I hired what I thought was a reputable company to do the work. In the following months, when a few problems arose with the electric, I discovered that the company had gone out of business and was nowhere to be found. Finally, the electric and other problems were taken care of and the apartments had been rented.

The cash flow ended up at approximately $750 per month. This allowed me to pay down the principal quickly, and if needed, have extra money to take care of any major repairs. The property was purchased for $35, 000. I sank another $15,000 to 18,000 for repairs and renovations. Several years later I had the principal paid down to about $25,000 and decided to refinance the property because there was another property in my hometown that I was interested in. So, I refinanced the property for $60,000 and used the difference ($35,000) to pay cash for the new property. This amount enabled me to purchase and renovate a half double with two rental units. The positive cash flow for the new property was $800 per month. A few years thereafter, I sold the first property for $76,500.

The second property that I purchased was in the same year as the three-unit property. I was still green and ignorant. This was a single house with an extra lot. It was an older, but large, house that needed work. The purchase price was $35,000. I figured about $5-6,000 for the renovations. The biggest mistake that I made on this property was not re-checking the property on the day before settlement. When I first looked at the house, I thought I did a thorough job of inspecting and determining what had to be done. Of course, I turned on all of the faucets, flushed the toilet to check for pressure, etc.

However, from the time of first inspection to settlement, a couple of months passed. I did not check out the water the day before closing, and what had happened was that since the house was empty, and the water off, the lines had completely closed up. Old galvanized pipe tends to do that over the years. I was not able to get any water through the house. The sediment had dried and hardened throughout the system.

Always inspect the plumbing. If you find old galvanized pipes, rest assured that you will need to replace them sooner or later. From experience on other properties, I found that trying to 'repair' the galvanized pipes can lead to headaches as well. If you need to replace a joint or length of galvanized pipe, you'll find it best to replace all pipes and joints that you possibly can. Sometimes when one pipe is tightened, other pipes and joints come loose and begin to leak as well. Whenever you have old pipe that is exposed, take the time to replace it. This will save you time, money, and headaches in the future.

Fortunately for me, the water line to the house was in good condition, or I would have had that expense as well.

One concern for vacant property should be the condition of the water line and sewer line. Long periods of non-use normally cause problems. Have these checked out whenever possible before purchasing your investment property. If you purchase a property that has been vacant for an extended period, it will be worth the money to have the line "snaked" by a plumber to clear any roots or debris that might have lodged in the sewer line.

Soon after I purchased this property, I subdivided the lot, and sold the extra lot that came with the house. This helped to pay down the principal tremendously.

Besides this major error, the property has been fine overall through the years. Yes, there have been repairs (hot water heater, new roof, etc.), but for the most part, things have been great. In the eighteen years that I have owned the property, I have not lost one month of rent due to vacancy. The property has a good cash flow and is now paid off. The tenants finally decided to purchase a home of their own, so I completely rehabbed the property (cost about $ 25,000) and sold it for $ 139,000.

The next property I purchased was a half double. For reasons that I still don't know, the bank would not give me a loan on this property. This is when I began to use the equity in my personal home to my advantage. I obtained a home equity line of credit and used the money to purchase and renovate this new venture. Through a series of transactions, which included refinancing the house above, I was able to pay off my home equity loan, thus owning this half double free and clear. The significance of owning free and clear was the ability to sell this property to the existing tenant with me holding the mortgage. Now, instead of the bank making all the money on interest, I will be receiving payments for the next 15 years.

At other times, I have used the home equity loan to purchase properties, then once the property was renovated and rented, I took out a mortgage on the rental property and paid off my home equity loan. This enabled me to have funds available for the next purchase.

There have been times that I purchase a property strictly for the purpose of renovating then re-selling. The home equity was very helpful in that funds were available to me as they were needed. I did not have to go through a bank, paying application fees, attorney fees, points, etc. These fees add up in a hurry, and if you get to the point of buying several properties, the total of all fees will be quite substantial.

In between the purchase of property for investment (rental) purposes, I have, over the years, purchased property for the short term--property for renovation and immediate re-sale. This has worked out extremely well. Most of the properties are those that need extensive renovation but were ones that I believed had potential for a quick turn over and substantial profit. Such projects, however, will not fit into everyone's schedule. If you hire others to do all of the work, your profit will be substantially less and may not be worth the trouble. If you are able to do much of the work, your profit will be much higher. There is a price for doing your own work, though. When I first started, I still had my regular full-time job. This meant that any work done on the investment property would have to be done in the evenings and on the weekends. This can, and did, get old fast. It was difficult, but now that I am through it, I am glad I did. More recently, since I left my full-time job, I have

the time to work on the investment properties during normal working hours.

This has been much to my liking as well as to that of my wife and family.

I am able to work on my own schedule, enjoy what I'm doing, and make

a living besides. The short term properties have carried me while the

investment properties continue to gain equity and give me security for the

future. Many times, with the proceeds of the short term property, I have paid

down the principal of one of the investment properties. The sooner that I get

them paid for, the sooner I can stop making mortgage payments and pocket

the difference.

One example where paying down the mortgage helped was the time I

had a duplex for sale. The buyer did not want to put anything down out of

his pocket, and the bank wanted him to have at least 20% equity in the

property. Since I was able to have the mortgage paid down, I offered to take

back a second mortgage in the amount of 20% if the bank would give the

buyer a mortgage of 80%. This way the buyer did not have to come up with

any money down. I now have a note in which I receive regular monthly

payments of principal and interest from this property.

Does it seem to you that I am very interested in paying off the mortgage

as soon as possible? I hope so, because I certainly am. Why? The longer that

you take to pay off the loan, the more you pay in interest. You will not

believe the difference in the amount of interest a few to several years can make. In the next chapter, I will discuss amortization of your mortgage and give several examples of different time periods and rates of interest, and how it can take thousands of dollars out of your pocket, or put thousands into your pocket.

CHAPTER 9

AMORTIZATION

Amortize means extinguishing or reducing a debt by making payments. When we purchase a home or investment property perhaps the most meaningful number is the amount of our mortgage payment. We want to know how much this property is going to cost us each month in principal and interest. Sometimes upon request, a bank or lending institution will furnish you with a copy of the amortization schedule, which is a listing of all of your monthly payments for the term of your loan. The schedule will list the total payment, and then how each payment is divided into principal and interest.

With each monthly payment, the amount of interest becomes less, and the amount applied to principal increases. The amount of the decrease of interest and increase of principal is determined by the rate and the term of the loan. The shorter the term, the faster the amount of principal paid each month increases.

Let's take a look at the three examples that follow starting on page 81. Each amortization schedule is for the same loan amount ($60,000), but for different rates and/or terms. See the difference in the amount of interest that is paid for each schedule. The first example shows the loan of $60,000 at 7.5% with 180 monthly payments. One hundred eighty payments is a term of 15 years. Over the period of 15 years, you will have paid back the principal of $60,000 plus $40,116.90 in interest. Yes, you're right, that is a lot of interest to pay! However, look at the next example, and here the interest rate is moved up a little to 9%. At the end of 15 years, you again have paid the principal back, but this time the amount of interest is $49,540, over $9,400 more for the same term! How many ways can you think of to spend that extra $9,000 if you still had it?

Finally, look at the third example, which shows the same loan amount with a rate of 7.5% but this time with a term of 360 monthly payments. One advantage to extending the loan to 360 payments or 30 years is that your monthly payment will be less. This will give you a higher positive cash flow each month for the maintenance of the unit. Or it will give you extra money each month to do with as you so choose. Now, doesn't that sound good? Sure does! But, and there is a big BUT....the longer that you extend your loan, the more that you will be paying back in interest. How much more? Let's take a look.

In the first example of $60,000 at 7.5% for 15 years, you will remember that you will have paid a total of $40,116.90 in interest. Example #4 shows the first 14 payments and last ten payments for the same loan, but this time for 360 months instead of 180 months. Note the small amount of principal and the large amount of interest that is paid each month. Now look at the final figure in the interest column. The amount of interest that will be paid back over the term is $91,028.68. Compare this figure to the $40,116.40 in interest for the 15 year note, and you have a difference of approximately $51,000 extra that you will have paid! This is a substantial amount in anyone's book.

Even if you choose to pick the 30-year loan over the 15-year loan for whatever reason, there are ways to reduce the amount of interest that you will have to pay.

Even a small difference in interest rates can make a tremendous difference in the total amount that is paid back to the bank on your mortgage. Whenever possible, negotiate or shop around for the best interest rates. Sometimes you can obtain a better rate if you are willing to pay "points" up front. A point is a percentage of the loan amount. In our example of $60,000, one point would equal one percent of $60,000, or $600.

Choosing between paying points and a lower interest rate depends on how long you expect to keep the property. If you plan on keeping the property long term, then in most cases I would choose the lower rate with points because over the long run, the lower rate will save you more money. If, on the other hand, you plan to keep the property only a short time, you would be better off in most cases to pay the higher rate and avoid paying any points up front. I suggest taking a few minutes to do the calculation and project how much each rate will cost in interest over the years to determine whether or not you should take rates with points, or simply take the higher rate with no points.

Another way to reduce the amount of interest that you pay is to pay extra principal with your regular monthly payment. There are several ways to do this. Some institutions advertise a program that lets you pay bi-weekly payments instead of monthly. This will reduce the length of time that it takes to pay off your mortgage, thus saving you a substantial amount of interest to be paid over the course of your mortgage. This is a good program for those of you who may not be able to discipline yourself to make extra principal payments on your own each month. You are set up to make bi-weekly payments, and you will condition your budget for these payments. However, in most cases there is a fee of a few to several hundred dollars to be set up with this program. Then you may or may not be able to go back to monthly payments should you desire to in the future, without some sort of penalty or refinance charge.

Another way is to simply pay lump sum or random payments of additional principal to shorten the term of the loan, thus saving money in interest. This method may work best for those of you who are not paid on a regular basis such as weekly or bi-weekly. Or you may choose to pay a lump sum with an income tax refund or an unexpected windfall. This too will reduce the term, thus saving you money on the interest that was to be paid.

The method I use and the one that I show during my landlord classes is a little different. Refer to the amortization schedule of our example of $60,000 with a rate of 7.5% over a period of 360 months. (Example # 4) This time, let's concentrate on the payments themselves instead of the totals. Notice that payment #1 shows a total payment of $419.53. Of that amount, the interest is $375 and the principal is only $44.53. As you can see, early on in the mortgage, the principal payment is very low compared to the total amount of payment. At the end of the loan, the principal amount comes to be almost the entire portion of the total payment.

SO YOU WANT TO BE A LANDLORD
AMORTIZATION SCHEDULES

Example #1.

$60,000 on October 1 at 7.50% with 180 monthly payments

Date	Payment	Interest Amt.	Principal Amt.	Balance
11/01	556.21	375.00	181.21	59,818.79
12/01	556.21	373.87	182.334	59,636.45

Totals for 180 payments, or 15 years

	100,116.90	40,116.90	60,000.00	

Example #2.

$60,000 on October 1 at 9.00% with 180 monthly payments.

Date	Payment	Interest Amt.	Principal Amt.	Balance
11/01	608.56	450.00	158.56	59,841.44
12/01	608.56	448.81	159.75	59,681.69

Totals for 180 payments, or 15 years

	109,540.82	49,540.82	60,000.00	

Example #3.

$60,000 on October 1 at 7.50% with 360 monthly payments

Date	Payment	Interest Amt.	Principal Amt.	Balance
11/01	419.53	375.00	44.53	59,995.47
12/01	419.53	374.72	44.81	59,910.66

Totals for 360 payments, or 30 years:

	151,028.68	91,028.68	60,000.00	

Example #4.

$60,000 on October 1 at 7.50% with 360 monthly payments

Date	Payment	Interest Amt.	Principal Amt.	Balance
11/01	419.53	375.00	44.53	59,955.47
12/01	419.53	374.72	44.81	59,910.66
01/01	419.53	374.44	45.09	59,865.57
02/01	419.53	374.16	45.37	59,820.20
03/01	419.53	373.88	45.65	59,774.55
04/01	419.53	373.59	45.94	59,728.61
05/01	419.53	373.30	46.23	59,682.38
06/01	419.53	373.01	46.52	59,635.86
07/01	419.53	372.72	46.81	59,589.05
08/01	419.53	372.43	47.10	59,541.95
09/01	419.53	372.14	47.39	59,494.56
10/01	419.53	371.84	47.69	59,446.87
11/01	419.53	371.54	47.99	59,398.88
12/01	419.53	371.24	48.29	59,350.59

Below is listed the last ten payments of this mortgage. Notice how the principal amounts are nearly the total amount of the payment. Note that the following payments are assumed to occur thirty years after the previous list.

Date	Payment	Interest Amt.	Principal Amt.	Balance
01/01	419.53	25.33	394.20	3,658.42
02/01	419.53	22.87	396.66	3,261.76
03/01	419.53	20.39	399.14	2,862.62
04/01	419.53	17.89	401.64	2,460.98
05/01	419.53	15.38	404.15	2,056.83
06/01	419.53	12.86	406.67	1,650.16
07/01	419.53	10.31	409.22	1,240.94
08/01	419.53	7.76	411.77	829.17
09/01	419.53	5.18	414.35	414.82
10/01	417.41	2.59	414.82	0.00

Totals for Term of Mortgage: 151,028.68   60,000.00

I advise anyone who asks, to begin making extra principal payments as early in the loan as possible. My method is to pay extra by the exact amount of the next principal payment. As stated above, payment number one consists of $375 for interest and $44.53 in principal. Payment number two lists $44.81 as the principal payment. This is the amount of "extra" that I send along with payment number one. In essence, what I have accomplished is to eliminate one monthly payment from the term of my loan. Remember, each monthly payment is $419.53. So by paying the extra $44.81, I have eliminated a payment of $419.53 for a savings of $374.72. Now, you must continue to make a payment each month, but you have eliminated a payment at the end of your loan.

Suppose I wanted to eliminate two payments on the next scheduled mortgage payment (refer again to example # 4). Since we paid payment number one and the principal on payment number two, in the next scheduled payment, we would be paying payment number three. Here the interest is $374.44 and the principal is $45.09. Now, to eliminate two payments, I need to pay an extra $91.02 which is the total of the principal amounts in payments number four and five. So, by paying this extra $91.02, I will have eliminated two payments of $419.53 which totals $839.06 and a realization of $748.04 saved in interest. ($839.06 minus $91.02).

The nice thing about this method is that you can make as many or as few extra principal payments as you want. If you don't want to, or are unable to make an extra principal payment in a particular month, you don't have to. By paying the exact amount of extra principal instead of lump sums, you will know at all times exactly what your remaining balance is. Usually every three months when property taxes are due, I find that the positive cash flow does not permit me to pay too much extra, but during the other months, I can pay a good deal extra on principal.

Another key to taking the best advantage of this method is to *begin early* in the term of the mortgage. You can easily see that the principal amount increases each month, and by the latter stages of the term the principal amount is quite large. It will be more difficult to make extra payments when the principal amount approaches half or more of the entire payment amount. My goal was always to make as many extra payments during the first five years of the mortgage. You can eliminate more payments with less "extra" money earlier in the term of the loan than you can later in the term. Again, my goal has always been to eliminate debt as soon as possible. Trust me, it will come in handy and pay dividends in the future.

CHAPTER 10

EXPENSES

How many times have you heard the phrase "Don't worry, you can deduct that expense"? Although the statement is true in most cases, deductions, in reality, are a two-sided story. Yes, with income properties, you will have expenses which are deductible, and we will discuss them in this chapter. Yes, expenses will help lower the amount of taxes that you will be paying. But, expenses for deduction's sake are not worth all they are cranked up to be. Nevertheless, we are grateful for them as we prepare our tax returns, because they are helping us by reducing our tax.

If I could, I would rather do without the expenses as deductions and then gladly pay the extra tax that would be due. The reason is that, depending on your tax bracket, a $100 expense that is deductible may result in a tax savings of $15 to $30 dollars. Better to pay the tax. However, as I mentioned, we will have expenses that are deductible, so let's make the best use of them.

First of all, let me say this. ***KEEP ACCURATE AND DETAILED***

RECORDS! It's okay to become a fanatic about saving receipts for all of

your investment properties. If you do nothing more than to accumulate all

your receipts in a shoe box (a separate box for each property of course), great.

But if you hand these to your accountant this way, you may find that the extra

time that the accountant spends sorting through the records will cost you

dearly.

Each of you will have your own method of keeping records. You may

organize your records on a weekly, monthly, quarterly, or whatever basis.

Personally, I use a separate spreadsheet for each property. I have developed

the habit of organizing my receipts at the end of the year only. It is probably

not the best method, but it works for me. Each January, I bite the bullet and

spend many hours sifting through my business checkbook and placing the

check with the appropriate property. Cash slips are placed in files by property

and then totaled at the end of the year. It is highly recommended that you

keep a separate checking account for your rental business.

The Internal Revenue Service uses schedule 'E ' to list rental income and

expenses for your investment properties. At the end of this chapter you will

find a sample that I have prepared from a property that I owned in the past.

On this form, each rental property is listed by address and type of

building (single family, duplex, etc.). In the income section, we list the total

amount of rents received. During the year, as I collect the rents for the various properties, I mark in the stub area of my checkbook the name and address of the property for which the rent was received. At the end of the year, I make a separate spreadsheet just for rents, listed by property. This will give me a handy reference for the total rents received for all of the properties.

Next, you will see the expense area which has a number of different categories. The advertising expense will be for any newspaper or other advertisements that were used to promote your property for rent or for sale. Any form of advertising that can be verified can be incorporated in this line.

Auto and travel expense. This expense is often overlooked. My first accountant never asked me about this, and since I didn't know about it, I lost several hundred dollars over the few years that I used this particular accountant. Now I keep a notebook in my truck and write down the beginning and ending mileage each day. I make a note of where I went and for which property. You can deduct mileage for traveling to the property itself as well as mileage for running to the hardware or supply store to pick up the necessary materials for each property. The allowance for mileage changes each year and can be a substantial deduction. Also, expenses such as insurance and auto repairs are deductible as well. These expenses are deducted at a rate depending on the percentage of use that your particular vehicle is used for the rental business.

Cleaning and maintenance. If you hire someone to clean your apartment or maintain it in any way, this expense is deductible. Personally, I clean, repaint and maintain my own units. When I first started, I did not have the extra funds to hire someone else. Now I have the time to do it myself, so I save the expense of hiring someone else. This would be a good time to mention that any cleaning, maintenance work, or repair work that you do yourself is not deductible. If you hire someone to do the work, then you can claim the expense. If you do it yourself, you cannot claim any labor as a deduction.

Commissions. If you have a rental agency secure tenants for you, there is usually a charge to you. This charge or commission is a deductible expense. A common charge in my area is one half the first month's rent, and 10% for each month thereafter for "managing" the property. .

Insurance. The liability and fire insurance that you have to protect yourself and your property is deductible. I would advise shopping around for the best rates versus coverage. I would also advise securing the highest level of liability that is within reason. Although I have never had a claim against my insurance, trying to maintain a property without insurance is a "no-no".

Legal and other professional fees are fees that may be incurred by the use of an attorney, courthouse fees, consulting fees for the rental property, etc. Your accounting fee could be entered here as well.

Management fees. Some of you will find that hiring a manager is good. You may not want to invest the time to manage properties yourself for various reasons. If you have the cash flow and you have several units, a property manager may work out just fine. I have always managed my own properties, but there are times that I thought to myself that it sure would be nice to have someone else handling these for me. Usually the beginner does not have the extra funds to pay someone else to manage their unit or units. These fees can take a substantial part of your cash flow, and even though they are deductible, remember $1,000 in fees saves only $150 to $350 in taxes, depending on your tax bracket.

Mortgage interest paid to banks. This is the amount of interest that you pay each year on your mortgage for the property. This is usually a substantial amount, especially in the early years of your mortgage. Again, although it is a nice deduction, it is still better to pay off your loan as soon as possible. Every extra principal payment will lessen the amount of interest that you will have to pay. Consider this: if your bank pay 3% or 4% for CD's, and 1% for savings, and your mortgage rate is 7%, where are you really saving more money?

Other Interest. This amount is usually for money you borrowed to maintain your unit. Or perhaps you used your credit card to buy supplies and you are charged interest on this amount.

Repairs. Repairs that you make to your property such as fixing the floor, wall, windows, new faucet, etc. are deductible, if you are paying someone else to do the work. If you do it yourself, then it is not deductible. Common repairs include heater repairs, plumbing, replacing an electrical outlet. Major repairs such as a new roof and new windows may fall under another category called improvements. These expenses are treated differently from the common repair. These are not deducted in the same fashion on schedule E. However, you will be able to use the cost of these improvements to your advantage. Publication 17 of the IRS Code gives examples of repairs versus improvements. The cost of the improvements is deducted or "depreciated" over a longer period of time and will be a help when you sell your investment property. Please see your accountant for help in this area.

Supplies are simply the cost of the materials that are used to make repairs in your unit. Keep all receipts, even for the items that do not cost very much. I call these 'pocket change' items. You will be surprised how much they accumulate over the course of the year.

Taxes. The dreaded property tax is totally deductible. Depending on your area of the country and then the particular area of your property, this expense will be substantial as well.

Utilities. These costs could include your heat and hot water expense if you include it in the rent, water and sewer charges, and electric, if included in the rent. Tenant-paid utilities are not deductible. If your unit is heated by oil, and you have the tank filled in whole or in part to start the tenant off, then the portion that you pay for is deductible.

Other. This line is for any miscellaneous items that may not fall in any of the above categories.

The next section tells you to add up all of the expenses and place the total on the line. The following line is for the depreciation expense. This deduction is a good short-term helper, but it will catch up to you when you sell your investment property. For example, if you purchase a property for $54,000, the depreciate deduction is equal to approximately 1/27th of the cost each year. For this property of $54,000 the deduction would be $2,000 per year (1/27th of the cost of the house). Once the depreciation is calculated, it is placed on the appropriate line on schedule E and is added to the expenses line above it to get the total expenses.

Finally, you take your total expenses and subtract it from the total rents to determine if you have an income or loss for each property. If you have more than one property, these lines are totaled and placed on the appropriate line on form 1040.

The above is simply a general 'walk through' of schedule E. I cannot overemphasize the importance of consulting with a qualified accountant on some of these matters. Finding a good accountant is finding one who earns his or her pay by maximizing allowable deductions and minimizing the amount of tax due.

If schedule E shows a loss, it's not the end of the world. It may be because of the depreciation expense that you are showing a 'paper loss'. A quick way to determine if you actually had a profit or loss is simply to take all of your out-of-pocket expenses (line 19) and subtract them from your rents received. Don't overlook your equity gain on your mortgage. I take the amount I paid in principal for the year, add it to my total rents, then subtract the expenses. This gives a fairly true picture of what you actually are making for the year on each property.

SCHEDULE 'E'

(Income and Loss from rental real estate)

Below you will find the general thrust of schedule 'E' from the Internal Revenue Service. There are other lines that need to be completed when you file these forms. Your accountant can review these forms with you at the time of filing each year. Each form is set up to list as many as three properties, but for the sake of example, I will show only one.

Part I. Show the kind and location of each rental property.

(Single family, duplex, tri-plex, etc.) and the property address

For our example: duplex, 2 units, 123 Main Street, Anytown, NJ

Income: Rents received. On this line you are to list the total rents received for this property.

Total rents: $10,400.00

Expenses:

Advertising	$48.00
Auto and Travel	$90.00
Clean and maintenance	$200.00
Commissions	$0.00
Insurance	$590.00
Legal/Professional fees	$100.00
Management fees	$0.00
Mortgage Interest	$3600.00
Other Interest	$0.00
Repairs	$375.00
Supplies	$285.00

Taxes	$1900.00
Utilities	$960.00
Other (list)	$49.00
Add all of the above expenses	$8148.00

**At this point you show a gain of $2252.00, which is the difference between the total rents received and the total of expenses. However, there is an additional benefit on the next line of depreciation expense.

Depreciation expense	$2000.00
Total Expenses	$10,148.00
(above expenses plus depreciation)	
Income or (loss)	$252.00

(this is the amount of income on which you pay tax)

(Total rents $10,400 less total expenses)

CHAPTER 11

THE CAPITAL GAINS TAX AND 1031 LIKE KIND EXCHANGES

This may be the shortest chapter in the book because as I mentioned before, I am not an accountant. I just want to mention these topics in passing. Please consult your accountant for further and detailed information.

The capital gains tax, in my opinion, is the worst enemy to true economic stability and a long standing robust economy, and the enemy of lower income taxes for all Americans.

Many years ago, the tax rate was 33% or more in most cases. In 1998, the rates were lowered in a lot of cases, sometimes to as low as 15%. This was a step in the right direction and did much to stimulate the economy.

Other aspects of this tax have changed as well. Changes have occurred concerning one's principal residence. In previous years, you could take a one time capital gains exclusion if you sold your home and were over the age of 55. Now, the one-time exclusion has been repealed and couples can take an exclusion on the sale of any home in which they have resided for two of the last five years. This exclusion can be used over and over again.

The holding period for assets or investment property has changed in order for them to qualify for capital gains treatment.

We still have a long way to go. It is my *opinion* that, should the capital gains tax be eliminated, the economy would grow as never before. So many people would be working that the tax base would be increased to the point that even the income tax could be reduced (assuming of course that government stops finding ways to spend it). Let me add that not only am I not an accountant, I am not a politician, nor am I an economist--just an average individual trying to make a living and prepare for retirement and the future of my children. So feel free to ignore my opinion if you like.

The reason I believe that the capital gains tax hurts the economy is that the tax actually discourages investors and businesses from growing and multiplying their businesses. The capital gains tax is such a huge portion of an investor's profit that many investors who might invest or expand on a regular basis, decide to place their money elsewhere, such as in the stock market, in savings, or in some other safe haven.

In a nutshell, the capital gains tax is a tax on the profit as a result of the sale of your property. If you purchased a property today for $80,000 and sold it for $100,000, you are liable for a tax on $20,000 which is the difference between the purchase price and selling price. Depending on your tax bracket, the tax could be as high as 33% or approximately $6,700.

Now let's say that you purchased the property 10 years ago for $80,000 and you sold it this past year for $100,000. Your profit is still $20,000. However, your capital gains tax is based on a figure much higher than the $20,000. Remember our discussion of depreciation in a previous chapter? Well, in our pending example, you have been depreciating your $80,000 property over the last ten years at approximately $3,000 per year. This has helped you each year to reduce the tax that was due. Over the last 10 years, you have depreciated your property by $30,000. Now when it comes time to figure your capital gains tax, the IRS sees a property purchased at $80,000, depreciated $30,000 for a new base figure of $50,000, then a selling price of $100,000. Now you must pay the capital gains tax on $50,000, which is the difference between the new 'base' price of $50,000 and the selling price of $100,000. Ouch!

Some may ask, "What's the big deal anyway?" These investors are making huge profits; they should be taxed on their gain! Yes, there are gains, and sometimes they are substantial. But as an investor, if my profits are taxed heavily, then I have less to invest in the next project or business. Each time I scale down or forego another investment, I fail to provide as many or any jobs at all. Each time I buy a property for investment, I usually end up hiring an electrician, roofer, and drywall contractor to mention a few. Sometimes I rent a dumpster which helps to keep someone busy. I buy materials from local businesses, such as plumbing, lumber, and electrical. All of these businesses and contractors have work because of my investment. As these contractors work and businesses sell me their goods, earnings are made and sales are produced. And as work is done, income is produced and yes, more taxes are paid as a result of the additional income. The investor also will pay additional tax on the gain. The Federal, State, and local governments all benefit from increased production.

The more incentive the government can give in the form of lower taxes to business and investors, the more the government will benefit in the long run. Yes, businesses and investors will continue to make money, perhaps quite a bit of money. However, it is these same businesses and investors that create the jobs for the work force. Without them, the economy will crumble. Without growth, jobs are lost, unemployment rises, the tax base erodes, and higher taxes result on those still working. Enough said.

CHAPTER 12

THE APPLICATION

The rental application does not have to be a complex document.

However, there are several important bits of information that you should

require of your applicants. The more information that you can get from your

prospective tenants, the better. Design the application to fit your particular

needs. Below is a sample application that I have used in the past. Any of you

are free to use this sample if it is a help to you.

RENTAL APPLICATION

NAME_____

PHONE_____

EMAIL_____

ADDRESS_____

HOW LONG AT CURRENT ADDRESS_____

PREVIOUS ADDRESS (IF LESS THAN 2 YEARS)

_____

PLACE OF EMPLOYMENT

_____

ADDRESS_____

PHONE_____

HOW LONG_____WAGE/SALARY_____

PREVIOUS EMPLOYER (IF LESS THAN 2 YEARS)

_____

ADDRESS AND PHONE

_____

OTHER INCOME_____

DATE OF BIRTH_____

SOCIAL SECURITY_____

DRIVERS LICENSE NUMBER

_____

LANDLORD'S NAME, ADDRESS, PHONE

_____

PRESENT RENT_____

NAME / ADDRESS OF RELATIVE

_____

CO-APPLICANT

NAME_____

PHONE_____

ADDRESS_____

DATE OF BIRTH_____

SOCIAL SECURITY_____

EMPLOYER_____

HOW LONG_____

ADDRESS_____

PHONE_____WAGE/SALARY_____

PREVIOUS EMPLOYER (IF LESS THAN 2 YEARS)

_____

ADDRESS AND PHONE

_____

OTHER INCOME

_____

NAME AND ADDRESS OF RELATIVE

_____

CREDIT REFERENCES:

(LIST BANK LOANS, CREDIT CARDS, CHARGE ACCOUNTS, ETC)

_____

_____

_____

NAMES AND AGES OF THE PERSONS
TO BE LIVING IN THIS UNIT

_____

_____

WHEN COULD YOU BE READY TO MOVE INTO THIS UNIT?

_____

PLEASE NOTE: This unit will be shown on several dates within this week. After all of the showing dates, the applications will be processed. By_____, all the applications will be processed. You will be notified by phone if we can rent this unit to you. **PLEASE BE SURE** that you have listed all of your credit references. This is very important and is a main consideration in our decision to rent to you. Also, make sure that all questions are answered as fully as possible. <u>By signing this application, you are giving the owner permission to obtain a credit report</u>. Thank you. We appreciate your call and your time in viewing this unit.

YOUR SIGNATURE

_____

CO-APPLICANT SIGNATURE

_____

The obvious includes the name, address and phone number. It is important to have the phone number should you need to reach the applicant with further questions. Also, you may need to be able to contact the tenants when the need arises. If the applicant does not have a phone, a small caution flag should start waving. My experience with tenants who have no phone has indicated either a tremendous lack of income on their part or a desire to keep other creditors from reaching them. This is not always the case, but nevertheless, be aware.

If the current address is less than two years, I ask for a previous address. I try to establish residence for at least the past two years. If you have an applicant who shows residency for only a few or several months at a time, another caution flag is waving in the breeze. There may be good reason for the frequent moves, and you should inquire why. However, frequent moving could indicate evictions, or some other landlord/tenant problem. Many times I come right out and ask why the applicant is moving. Sometimes he says how awful his present landlord is, how he/she never takes care of anything. Usually there are two sides to this story as well, and it is in your best interest to get to the bottom of the issues if this particular applicant is one you intend to choose to occupy your unit. The very first prospective tenant whom I interviewed in my partnership property told me the reason that she was moving was because she was being evicted. I asked her why she was being evicted, and she told me that she was not paying the rent! I said "Okay then.

I don't think that we can be of any help to you. Thank you for stopping by...."

Employment history is important because it tells you something about the stability of the applicant. If your applicant changes jobs every few months, the caution flags are still flying. There is a stability problem here, and it will most likely become your problem if you allow this applicant to rent your unit. It is also important to verify the applicant's income so that you can determine if he or she is able to afford your apartment. Many times tenants either think that they can afford the rent and really can't, or are hoping that you can't figure and reason for yourself. If their monthly net income is less than twice the rent, you are likely to have problems collecting the money due to you each month. Try to verify the employment by telephone. Sometimes employers will require you to submit a letter of request before they will give out any information. DO CHECK with the employer. You would be surprised at how many applicants give false information.

The date of birth and social security number are important because they allow you to check credit information. You must have written permission to run a credit check. I have a paragraph which tells the applicants, that by signing this application, they give me permission to obtain credit information. The more references that you can obtain, the better. If an applicant pays his bills on time, the chances are good that he will pay you the rent on time as well. If an applicant has no credit at all, one of two things is true. He either has no credit as stated, or he has no credit that he wants to tell you about. Sometimes I will take a chance on an individual or couple with no credit. Hey, we all need a break sometime, and if there is no derogatory credit on a particular applicant, then I will usually give him an opportunity. If applicants say they have no credit when they really have lots of credit and it is all bad, I will pass them by---and so should you.

Request driver's license, type of car, and tag numbers for future reference. You may need to track these people down at a later time, or you may want to keep track of who is parking in your yard. Also, find out who some of the close relatives are in the area and obtain their addresses and phone numbers. These will be handy references should you need to trace or locate your tenant in the event that he leaves and you want to find him for whatever reason.

I also request the present landlord's name and number as well. Personally, I don't put a lot of stock in the information that I get from the present landlord. Sometimes it is a family member who will give you an inflated reference. It might be a landlord who can't wait to get rid of this tenant because of problems, and the landlord might give you misleading information. If the tenant is a good tenant, the landlord may get upset at the fact that he is losing such a good tenant. Please understand that this is not always the case. I have found landlords that give accurate and honest information. I'm just saying, be a little cautious.

I ask for the present amount of rent the tenant is paying. If the rent he is paying and the rent you are asking for your unit are similar, then get a copy of his rent receipts and canceled checks. He should be able to pay your rent on time as well. If there is a big difference in the two amounts (yours being higher), then do a lot of figuring and ask a lot of questions to determine if the applicant will be able to pay your rent.

Always get the names and ages of the people who want to live in this unit. The local housing department will let you know the legal occupancy of your unit. Be sure that your applicants will not exceed the legal occupancy. This list will also help you in the event that you find several more people have moved into your unit and you have to have some of them removed.

One time I rented to a single mom who had two children. The unit was a small two bedroom apartment. Two months later, there were four children in the apartment. She said that she had gained custody of her two other children (ones I did not know about). The legal occupancy was now exceeded, and she promised that she would be looking for another larger unit. A couple of months went by and she was still in the unit. Four young children running around in a relatively small unit created 'abnormal' wear and tear. She continued to assure me that she was still looking for another apartment. The next month, her boyfriend and his two kids moved in. Enough was enough, and I had to threaten eviction. I actually had to file the papers, and they waited until the day before court to move out. By that time, rent was past due, and damages to the apartment were considerable.

Whenever I had a unit that was vacant and available, I would put an ad in one or two of the local newspapers for an apartment/house for rent. I use a three-line advertisement saying a little about the apartment including the rent amount. The amount of rent is included to eliminate calls from tenants who are not able or not willing to pay the amount of rent requested.

In my early rental experience, once an ad was placed and calls started to come in, I would ask the callers to tell me a convenient time that we could meet to see the unit. I soon found that I was running over to the unit at all times of the day and evening. Most of the time the callers came as agreed, but there were several times that they just did not show up. That used to aggravate me royally because not only did they not keep their appointment, but I considered it rude and inconsiderate, not to mention a waste of my time. Soon after, and ever since, when calls come in, I tell the candidates when I will be at the unit. I may give three different times on different days to accommodate various schedules. For example, I say that I will be there on Monday from 6pm to 7pm, Wednesday 9am to 9:30am, and Saturday 12 noon to 1pm. Usually applicants can come at one of these times. There are occasions when you have to make exceptions. Sometimes I will try to pre-screen these exceptions over the phone to determine if it is worth the time to make a special trip.

While at the apartment, I provide applications for anyone who desires to fill one out. I usually take a book to read while there in case no one shows, or, if there are small repairs, touch ups, or any final cleaning to do, I will use that time to finish the odds and ends instead of making another trip.

Depending on the unit location and size, you may have a few to several applicants or perhaps a few dozen. It has been my experience that the number of applicants does not dictate the quality. In other words, you may find a desired tenant from a pool of only three or four, or it may take a pool of 15 or more to come up with a qualified tenant. There have been times when the best qualified applicant was the first to see the apartment. Many times it has been the last applicant who was most qualified. There have also been times when, after having advertised the unit for two weeks, none of the applicants were ones whom I would have chosen to rent the unit. In that case, I simply ran the advertisement for a couple more weeks until I found someone with whom I felt comfortable and who was qualified.

Don't fret if you find yourself taking a little longer to find the applicant that you would be happy renting to. Oftentimes, a quick, rash decision will end up costing you big time in the long run. I know an empty apartment pays no rent. And I know that we can never make up rent for lost time or money for a vacant apartment. I also know that putting the wrong tenant in the unit for the wrong reasons will eventually cost you more than having the unit vacant for a few extra weeks.

Beware of the applicant who is too anxious. I have had many applicants bring cash to the apartment when they come to view the unit. They are ready to hand it over to you at that moment. My advice is don't take it! Wait until you have had a chance to properly screen the applicant.

I consider myself to be a kind, thoughtful person who wants to help others when they could use help. There have been many times that applicants have come to me with hard luck stories, and I wanted to help them into the unit, but I had to step back a little, use wisdom, and not get personally involved, because if I had rented to these people, it would have been a problem waiting to happen. Their dire circumstances would follow them to my unit, and before long, we would all be caught in a financial problem.

Keep in mind that there can be extenuating circumstances about an applicant that you should consider. Failure to do so may cause you to lose a good tenant. For example, unpaid medical bills may not necessarily indicate how a tenant is able to pay the day to day bills. Expensive health care costs can take a long time to pay or even settle with insurance companies.

If an applicant has been recently divorced, or is in the process of a divorce, credit problems may show up because of failure of a spouse to pay bills or credit cards. The best advice here is to check the credit "history" of the applicant.

If you are renting to roommates, make sure that each qualifies on his own. Make each aware that individually each is liable for rent in the event that one moves out.

Once I have all the applications in hand, my personal process of selecting a tenant is fairly simple. Usually, you can eliminate about 60% of the applications because of insufficient income, job instability, or residence instability. Before I go any farther, let me say that you cannot discriminate on the basis of race, sex, religion. Doing so will create problems that you do not want to incur.

Next, I take the remaining applications and look for credit references and good employment history, and I begin to make as many calls as possible to verify the information that was given. If I find any false information concerning the employment, I put that application aside. I have had tenants tell me they work for ABC Corporation only to find out that ABC Corporation has never heard of them. Sometimes the tenant exaggerates the income or length of time on the job. If you can't verify this information over the phone, call the applicant and ask for some recent pay stubs.

Then I will examine the applications for credit history. Each landlord will do things differently. I choose what I perceive to be the top three applicants, then do a credit check on all three. If you have access to the credit bureau, use it. Landlord Protect, or similar credit agencies, are an excellent means of checking the rental history and credit worthiness of an applicant. There is a cost for this service as well, but it is worth it. I also check with my local courthouse to determine if there are any small claims or landlord/tenant claims against the individuals. My worst nightmare of a tenant was one whose credit I had checked with the regular credit bureau. I found only a couple of charges for $100 or so that were delinquent, but none of the landlord tenant cases were on the report for some reason. I found out afterward, that had I spent a few minutes at the courthouse, I would have saved myself a couple of thousand dollars and a tremendous amount of aggravation. She had a list of claims as long as my arm! The county courthouse can provide you with information concerning any small claims or landlord/tenant cases on prospective tenants.

Some landlords charge to take an application and may or may not credit the charge to the applicant's rent if he is chosen for the unit. Personally, I do not charge for the application, but I do see the point in the charge. The charge will weed out any applicant who is not really interested in the unit. In the past, I have had applicants whom I felt comfortable with, called them to say that they were accepted and could rent the unit, only to have them tell me they were not interested anymore. That can be frustrating. The charge for the application also defers the money that you will spend to have the credit checked. I can't give you a convincing argument as to why I do not charge except that I feel comfortable not charging, and I am willing to absorb the cost.

After having chosen the 'top three' and checked them out as much as possible, I rate them 1,2,3. As one last step, I ride by the existing apartment of each of the top applicants to casually browse around the property looking for signs that might suggest how the applicant will keep my property once he has moved in. My excuse for showing up unannounced is that I need to have additional information for the application before the final decision. You can look around the inside without being obvious. If you see a neat and tidy apartment, you can expect the applicant to keep your unit the same way. If, on the other hand you see things that you do not like, expect those same things to show up on your property as well.

After these inspections, I call the applicant whom I feel is the strongest or best candidate for the rental unit. If still interested in the unit, then it is his. If not, I go to the next strongest candidate, and so on. As soon as one of the applicants says that he wants the unit, I ask for part of the security deposit (about one half), which is not refundable if he changes his mind between the time of acceptance and the actual move in time. I had one or two instances where the applicant said he wanted the unit, only to change his mind in the next day or so. Sometimes this will cause you to lose your other candidates to other apartments, and you may have to begin the process all over again.

Following is a simple form for the "Security Deposit to Hold an Apartment." This is easy to read and simple to understand. If a tenant is not willing to give you this deposit, he most likely is not committed to or interested in the unit.

DEPOSIT TAKEN TO RESERVE DWELLING UNIT

DATE_____

On the above date, (name of tenant) has given a deposit in the amount of _____ to reserve the dwelling located at

_____.

This deposit is to be applied to the total deposit required to rent the dwelling at the above mentioned address.

It is also understood, that, should the tenant change their mind about renting this dwelling, this deposit is non- refundable.

By signing below, I consent that I /we agree to and understand the statements above.

_____

TENANT   DATE

_____

TENANT   DATE

_____

LANDLORD   DATE

CHAPTER 13

SECTION 8

Section 8 rental assistance is a government funded program that helps prospective tenants find and pay for rental units. Income level and special needs are some of the qualifications that determine if individuals and families are eligible. Once on the program, the applicant looks for a suitable rental unit. As soon as a unit is found, the tenant will give you the name and number of the case worker involved. You have the right to screen these applicants just as you would any other applicant. If you decide to rent to an applicant on Section 8, and inspection of your unit is conducted to verify the number of bedrooms, check for any safety violations, note which appliances are included, and determine which utilities if any, are included.

The amount of rent that you can charge depends on the size of the apartment, the number of utilities that are included, and the area. You will enter into a separate lease (in addition to your lease) with the Section 8 office, and you will be required to have an annual inspection, which is in addition to any inspection from your municipality.

The office will ask you what the asking rent for your unit is, and if falls within the guidelines for the rent permitted for units of your size, then the amount will be granted. Usually, the rents permitted for Section 8 are higher than the rent you may be able to ask on the open market. Again, amount of rent is determined by size, which utilities are included, appliances included, and location. It would be a good idea to call the local office ahead of time to check the allowable rent for your size unit.

One advantage that attracts landlords is that most, or sometimes nearly all, of the rent due is mailed directly to the landlord from the state. When you enter into a lease with a Section 8 recipient, you will be informed of the portion of rent that will be paid by the state, and the portion for which the tenant is responsible. I know landlords who rent exclusively to Section 8 recipients. In the past I have rented to some Section 8 tenants. I've had good success with this program in some instances. On the other hand, some of the tenants have not worked out so well. For more information on this program you can contact the Section 8 Rental Assistance Program in your state.

CHAPTER 14

THE LEASE

Once you have chosen a candidate for your unit, you will need to review

the lease with them for the apartment or house. The lease can be as involved

or as simple as you desire, but you need to cover as many of the bases as

possible. My lease started out as one page, but over the years has increased to

nearly four pages (double-spaced). Many of the terms in my lease were

borrowed from other leases that my friends or fellow landlords use. It is a

good idea to read as many different leases that you can to find terms and

conditions that you feel will be beneficial to you. Some terms and conditions

were added because of circumstances or problems that developed over the

years as a result of my landlord experience.

Your lease will include terms that are required, and those that are

preferred by you. Let's look at some of the required terms first. Below you will see a copy of the lease that I use for my rental units. Feel free to use any

or all of this lease, adding or subtracting as you feel best.

LEASE AGREEMENT

DATED_____

    This agreement is between _____,
owners, and _____ tenant(s), for the dwelling
located at _____. Tenants agree to
rent this dwelling for _____per month, payable in advance on
the 1st day of the month. The first month's rent for this dwelling is
_____. The security/cleaning deposit is _____.
The deposit is refundable if the tenant(s) leave the dwelling clean, undamaged,
and free of personal belongings and debris. The deposit will be placed in an
interest bearing escrow account located at

_____.

    A deposit of _____ for _____ keys will
be refunded after the keys have been returned.

    If the rent payments are made by check, the check should be made
payable to _____. If
payment is made after the 5th of the month, a late fee of $25.00 will be added
to the rent due. If payment is made after the 12th, a late fee of $50.00 shall
be assessed. If payments are not received by the 15th of the month, eviction
proceedings will begin.

    Tenants will give 60 days notice in writing before they move and will be
responsible for paying rent through the end of this period, or when another
tenant approved by the owners has moved in, whichever comes first.

    Owners will refund all deposits within 30 days after tenants have moved
out completely and return their keys.

_____INITIAL

Only the following persons are to live in this dwelling:

List the names and ages:

_____

_____

_____

TENANTS AGREE TO THE FOLLOWING:

1. The length of this agreement shall be 12 months.

2. The dwelling may not be sublet or assigned.

3. The security deposit cannot be used as the last month's rent.

4. To keep yards and garbage areas clean.

5. To keep from making loud noises and disturbances.

6. Not to use the dwelling for any business, professional, unlawful, or hazardous purpose.

7. Not to allow the dwelling to be vacant for extended periods of time.

8. Not to paint or alter their dwelling without first getting written permission from the owners.

9. To park their vehicles in assigned areas, and to keep space free of oil drippings.

10. Not to keep liquid filled furniture in this dwelling.

11. To allow owners to inspect this dwelling, and to show it to prospective tenants or buyers at any and all reasonable times.

12. To pay rent by check or money order payable to the owners. Returned checks must be redeemed immediately, and a charge of $25.00 shall be assessed.

_____INITIAL

13. To pay for repairs of all damages, including drain stoppages they or their guests may have caused. Also, other damages including damages to appliances, fixtures, walls, structure, carpet, tile, are the responsibility of the tenants.

14. If the dwelling is heated by oil, tenant must supply owner with the name of the oil company that is being used. Tenant agrees to keep a substantial amount of oil in the tank because allowing the tank to run low will result is dirt being drawn into the system. Tenant will be responsible for service calls that are a result of oil running out and dirty oil being used.

15. Electrical service is adequate for the existing fixtures. If tenant owned appliances overload the present system, tenant is responsible for making service additions.

16. The landlord is not liable for any inconvenience or harm caused by any stoppage or reduction of services beyond the landlord's control. This does not excuse the tenant from paying rent or the landlord from promptly taking corrective action.

17. The tenant agrees to pay for any broken windows while they live in this unit.

18. Kerosene heaters are not permitted.

19. Trash removal is the responsibility of the tenants (set out trash on appropriate day).

20. Pets are not permitted.

21. Bills for damages must be paid by the tenant at the time of repair. If the landlord does the actual repair work, labor will be calculated at

_____ per hour. Evenings and weekends will be at the rate of _____.

22. Tenant has inspected the dwelling, and accepts it in its "as is" condition.

_____INITIAL

23. The landlord shall pay for minimum water and sewer charges.

24. Tenant will be responsible for any removal and safety precaution regarding ice and snow on steps and sidewalks and any other area of the premises.

25. Tenant agrees to comply with any municipal rules and regulations regarding trash and debris collection and placement of same.

26. Tenant is urged to obtain tenant's/renter's insurance to cover any damage to their personal property that may occur through the term of this lease.

27. The tenant acknowledges that the owner has installed smoke detectors that are in operational order. Tenant agrees to test the detectors periodically and replace the battery when needed. Tenant agrees that when the term of the lease is expired, they will leave the smoke detector in operational condition.

28. The tenant agrees to quit and surrender the premises whenever and for whatever reason this lease is terminated, and shall surrender in the SAME condition as it is now, except for normal wear.

29. Tenants shall be liable for all legal fees, attorney fees, and court costs in the event the landlord must take legal action against the tenant for violating any of the stipulations of the lease.

30. Any additional conditions/changes in the lease must be made in writing.

31. Additions/special conditions:

32. MEGAN'S LAW STATEMENT:

Under New Jersey Law, the county prosecutor determines whether and how to provide notice of the presence of convicted sex offenders in an area. In their professional capacity, real estate licensees or landlords are not entitled to notification by the county prosecutor under Megan's Law and are unable to obtain such information for you. The county prosecutor may be contacted for such further information that can be disclosed to you.

_____INITIAL

33. Violation of any part of this agreement, or non-payment of rent when due, shall be cause for eviction under the appropriate section of the applicable code, and the prevailing party shall recover court costs and reasonable attorney fees involved.

34. Tenants hereby acknowledge that they have read this agreement, understand it, agree to it, and have been given a copy.

Validity of Lease: If a clause or provision of this lease is legally invalid, the rest of this lease remains in effect.

SIGNED:

_____

OWNER   TENANT   DATE

_____

OWNER   TENANT   DATE

On my first page I include my name, the tenant's name, and the property that he will be renting. Next is the amount of rent per month and the date that the rent is due. The security/ cleaning deposit is then typed in. The reason I call it a security/cleaning deposit is to make it clear that I expect to have the unit returned to me in the same condition in which I rented it to the tenant. Many times the tenant will overlook this fact, and I let him know up front that part of his deposit will be used to have the unit cleaned if he fails to do so.

You must let the tenant know where you are holding his security deposit, and the deposit must be in a separate account from your general account. You cannot co mingle the funds. The security deposit must be maintained separately in an interest bearing account.

I charge a token deposit as an incentive to have the keys returned when the tenant leaves the unit. I change the locks between tenants but would like to have the keys returned so that I can use the lock on another unit in the future.

I state that if the rent is paid by check, it should be payable to me, and if the check is returned, there is a returned check fee of $25. If the rent, which is due on the first of the month, is not paid by the fifth, then the late charge is $25. If the rent is not paid by the 12th of the month, then the late charge becomes $50. My reasoning for two late charges is to encourage tenants to pay as soon as possible. If the rent is not paid by the 5th, there is still incentive to have the rent paid by the 12th. Without the second late charge, tenants might feel that there is no rush after the 5th, and who knows when the rent might be paid.

I then state that if the rent is not received by the 15th, eviction proceedings will begin. By this I mean that papers will be filed with the courthouse for a future hearing date. This procedure will be discussed further in the chapter "Here Comes the Judge".

I tell the tenants that they must give me a 60-day notice in writing before they move out of the apartment. Many leases simply state that a 30-day notice is needed, but the 60-day notice will give me more time to advertise and find a new tenant for the apartment, thereby, I hope, cutting down or eliminating any vacant period.

Refunds must be returned to the tenants within 30 days after they have moved out AND returned the keys. Tenants are not considered out until the keys have been returned.

It is also very important to have listed the names and ages of the people who will be occupying the unit. This will prevent (with some possible enforcement needed) others from moving in and staying illegally in your unit. I have not experienced this but have heard of situations where the original tenants decide they want to leave and have friends or family members take over the apartment without having the landlord know about it. If the names of the "new" tenants are not on your lease, you can have them evicted.

In New Jersey, Megan's Law statement and the lead based paint addendum are now included with the lease.

Megan's Law was passed as a result of the tragic death of a young girl who was murdered by a convicted sex offender who was living in her neighborhood. The identity of the offender was not known previous to the murder. Now, towns through the county prosecutor's office are notified if a convicted sex offender settles in the area. This statement in the lease indicates that as a landlord you are not entitled to such information and are unable to obtain any such information.

A sample of the statements and disclosures on the lead-based paint addendum is shown below. This disclosure form indicates if there are any records of lead base paint in the apartment or home. Both the landlord and the tenant must sign this form. Make two copies, keep one for yourself, and give the other to the tenant.

DISCLOSURE OF INFORMATION ON
LEAD-BASED AND/OR LEAD-BASED HAZARDS

Lead Warning Statement

Housing built before 1978 may contain lead-based paint. Lead from paint, paint chips, and dust can pose health hazards if not managed properly. Lead exposure is especially harmful to young children and pregnant women. Before renting pre-1978 housing, lessors must disclose the presence of known lead-based paint and/or lead-based paint hazards in the dwelling. Lessees must also receive a federally approved pamphlet on lead poisoning prevention.

Lessor's Disclosure

(a) Presence of lead-based paint and/or lead-based paint hazards (check I or II below)

(I)_____Known lead-based paint and/or lead-based paint hazards are present in the housing

(explain)_____

_____

(II)_____Lessor has no knowledge of lead-based paint and/or lead-based paint hazards in the housing.

(b) Records and reports available to the lessor (check I or II below)

(I) _____Lessor has provided the lessee with all available records and reports pertaining to lead-based paint and/or lead-based paint hazards in the housing (list documents below)

_____

_____

(II)_____Lessor has no reports or records pertaining to lead-based paint and/or lead-based paint hazards in the housing.

Lessee's Acknowledgment (initial)

(c)_____Lessee has received copies of all information listed above

(d)_____Lessee has received the pamphlet Protect Your Family from Lead in Your Home.

Certification of Accuracy

The following parties have reviewed the information above and certify, to the best of their knowledge, that the information they have provided is true and accurate.

_____

LESSOR   LESSEE   DATE

_____

LESSOR   LESSEE   DATE

As a landlord, you must also furnish the pamphlet entitled "Protect Your Family from Lead in Your Home". If a young child ingests paint chips containing lead and becomes sick with lead poisoning and you do not have the disclosure signed, nor have given the tenant the pamphlet, you could be in for a serious lawsuit. Cover the bases. <u>As much as possible.</u> **<u>Always.</u>**

Preferred terms can be as few or as many as you feel comfortable with. I will briefly discuss most of the terms that I have in my lease. Again, if they work for you, feel free to include them with your lease.

<u>1) The length of the agreement shall be twelve months.</u> Most landlords I know use this length. There are some that will accept a shorter term, but you really don't want to have to change tenants any more frequently than you have to. The more stability and longevity as far as tenant stay is concerned the better off you will be. This will minimize the number of times of going over to the apartment each time a tenant moves in and out, and will cut down on the vacancy rate for each unit.

<u>2) The dwelling may not be sublet or assigned.</u> As a landlord, you will be spending much time and energy screening applicants, trying to find the best possible tenant. You certainly do not want your tenant sub-letting or leasing the apartment to someone whom you probably will not even know or even care to have in your unit. Do not let the tenant move out and have the apartment rent taken over by someone else.

<u>3) The security deposit cannot be used as the last month's rent.</u> Many times, if the tenant knows that he will be leaving at the end of the month, he feels for some reason that the rent for the last month does not have to be paid since you are holding his security deposit. Not so, because you may need the deposit for cleaning, damages, rent, and late charges. You will be happy to return his deposit once he has moved out and have left the unit clean with all rent paid up to date.

4) To keep yards and garbage areas clean. Besides the obvious, this will keep your neighbors happy and keep local inspectors from sending you letters to have the yard cleaned up.

5) To keep from making loud noises and disturbances. Again, aside from the courtesy factor, this will keep the neighbors from calling you with complaints, and keep the police from having to visit your property because of the disturbances. Recently, my hometown passed an ordinance that is called the "Rowdy House" ordinance. If the police are called to the property three times and your tenants or their guests are cited for disturbances or are found guilty of criminal charges, you as a landlord must have them evicted or you will face a fine for each day that they remain in the unit.

6) Not to use the dwelling for any business, professional, unlawful, or hazardous purpose. You are renting a residential unit. That's what it should be used for. It certainly would be nice if the tenants did not do anything that would create a hazardous situation, nor violate the law, such as the use or sale of drugs. If you allow this to go on, you could possibly lose your property to the forfeiture law. That's right, your property could be seized by the government.

Once you discover an unlawful situation, advise the tenant immediately in writing, both by regular and certified mail, to cease and desist with the particular activity. If he continues, you can have him evicted. As long as you notify him and are working to correct the situation, the police will gladly work with you.

7) Not to allow the dwelling to be vacant for extended periods of time. If your tenants are going to be away for a considerable time (more than a few days), encourage them to let you know so that you are aware and can, perhaps, keep a closer eye on the property while they are away. This is to their benefit as well as yours.

8) Not to paint or alter their dwelling without first getting written permission. If my tenants want to paint their unit a different color, very rarely will I refuse them. As long as the color is not some wild, dark color, I will usually let them, especially if they have been in the unit for several years. I make it clear that I expect the unit to be returned to the original condition upon their leaving the apartment. I discourage wall paper because it is too hard to take off and repaint. Generally, if the alteration will improve the property, I will allow the tenant the freedom to decorate as he pleases. Even though it is my property, I want him to be comfortable in his home.

9) To park their vehicles in assigned areas, and to keep the space free of oil drippings. If your property consists of more than one unit, it is best to assign parking areas to eliminate any possible disagreements between tenants. Of course, they need to keep the areas clean.

10) Not to keep liquid filled furniture in the dwelling. Newer waterbeds have less water, and thus less weight. The older beds contained a tremendous amount of water that could possibly be a problem, especially if on the second floor and the beds leak. Your first floor will sustain damage as well, and if you have another tenant living downstairs, you now have a two tiered problem. If your property is an older unit, you might want to have the floor joist checked before allowing waterbeds because of the weight. Older homes usually have joists every twenty-four inches, and sometimes even farther apart. Newer construction places joists no further than 16 inches from center to center.

11) To allow the owners to inspect the dwelling, and to show it to prospective tenants or buyers at any and all reasonable times. I do not abuse this term. I always give my tenants at least 24 hours notice before coming into the unit, unless there is an emergency. I certainly respect their right to privacy, but at the same time, if they have given me notice that they will be vacating the property, I need to show the unit to other possible tenants as soon as possible to keep the vacancy time to a minimum. If the property is one that I have decided to sell, I will have to show the unit to any interested buyers.

12) To pay rent by check or money order. I prefer my tenants to pay by check. I furnish them with envelopes with my address so as to make it one step easier to send me the rent through the mail. Most tenants use the mail or bring me the rent themselves. I discourage tenants from having me go to the unit to pick up the rent, but I will certainly do it if necessary. If you find that you have a tenant who is habitually late, or you know of any other reason where it benefits you to take the time to get the rent yourself, by all means do it.

Returned checks must be redeemed immediately, and the return check charge is $25. The return check charge is pretty much standard. Make it high enough to discourage bad checks, because your bank will probably charge you, and you may have other checks written against the deposited check.

13) To pay for repairs of all damages or drain stoppages they or their guests may have caused. It is a good idea to have the tenants pay for any damages when you repair them and not to wait until they leave the unit and deduct these charges from their security deposit. You may find that the security deposit is not enough to cover cleaning, past due rent, and any damages. Drain (sewer) stoppages can occur when children who either live in the unit or are guests in the unit attempt to flush things that shouldn't be flushed in the toilet. Sometimes too much paper will cause a stoppage. These stoppages can usually be remedied with a plunger, but once in a while the ol' Roto Rooter is needed, and this service can be expensive.

14) Oil-heated units. The reason that I ask for the name of the oil supplier is two-fold. One, to be sure that tenants are not using a grade of oil that might cause problems with the fuel line, and two, to keep track, if necessary as to when the tenant puts oil in the tank. Several times I received calls from tenants saying the heater was not working. Almost always this was a result of the tenant letting the oil tank run dry. When they called for oil, all the dirt on the bottom of the tank was stirred, causing the nozzle to clog. A nozzle is inexpensive, but the service call is not. Tenants would swear that they had enough oil, and then I would find out that they had just called the oil company saying that they were out of oil, pointing me to the real problem. These service calls are the responsibility of the tenant. Tenants should be greatly encouraged not to allow the tank to run less than half full before ordering additional oil. In my lease, I make note of the amount of oil in the tank, and then require the tenant to replace the oil upon his departure,

15) Electrical Service. Especially if your apartment is an older property, tenants may overload the existing system by trying to use heaters, blow dryers, and other appliances at the same time or on the same circuits. You need to decide whether to update the service or to inform the tenants of any restrictions that might be necessary.

16) Disruption of services beyond the landlord's control. This simply means that there may be times when services are disrupted for whatever reason, and the tenants may be inconvenienced. You should certainly do everything possible to see that corrections are made as soon as possible, but sometimes things will take longer than you would like or have expected. The tenants are still responsible for rent during this time.

18) Broken windows Should be repaired as soon as possible and are certainly the responsibility of the tenant.

19) Kerosene heaters are not permitted and are not lawful. Tenants might think that this is a cheaper way of heating the unit, but they are not permitted in rentals and are dangerous for the tenants and your property. While on the subject of heaters, beware of the fact that a tenant who may not have money for the oil may be tempted to use the range for heat on occasions. This is terribly dangerous and will burn up your range before you know it.

20) Pets. My standard policy is no pets because of additional wear and tear. Carpets, doors, and trim may all be subject to pet abuse. I have on occasion permitted pets in some units. I have charged a "pet fee" of $25 per month to help cover any possible damage as a result of the pets. Each situation is different depending on the pet, the apartment, and the tenant. I would not want to lose an excellent tenant over this issue. I do know landlords, however, who adhere strictly to the no pet policy.

21) Bills for damages was mentioned in one of the terms above, but here I include some rates for work that I may have to do myself. This may or may not encourage a tenant to take care of some minor things himself.

22) Tenant inspection. Many landlords have a 'check in and check out' sheet where any damages or abnormalities are noted before the tenant actually moves in. In this way, each party is protected and has knowledge of anything that might need repair. When the tenant moves out, you should walk through the unit with him to point out any items that will need to be repaired or replaced. If he does not want to do these repairs, then let him know that the cost of the repairs will be deducted from the security deposit. Believe it or not, most tenants do not even bother to take the time to walk through with me at the termination of the lease. Take pictures before the tenant moves in and after the tenant vacates the unit. These pictures will prove to be valuable should your tenant contest the amount of security that is returned.

23) Minimum water and sewer. If your property is on the outskirts of town with no public water and sewer, you don't have to worry. In my town, there is a quarterly charge for sewer and a quarterly charge for water usage. I pay for the sewer which is a constant charge, and I also pay for the minimum water charge. The water charge varies depending on the amount used. Anything over the minimum charge is the responsibility of the tenant.

24) Snow removal from steps is the responsibility of the tenants.

25) Municipal trash removal rules. Tenants are to place trash in the proper area on the appropriate day. My town will not allow trash to be placed outside more than 24 hours ahead of the pickup time, and empty trash cans must be removed within 24 hours of pickup.

26) Renter's insurance. I advise my tenants to obtain renters insurance because the insurance that I purchase is for liability and fire on my property.

The tenant's belongings are not covered in the case of a loss. Renter's insurance is relatively inexpensive.

27) Smoke detectors. Before the tenant moves in, check to make sure that all of the smoke detectors have batteries and are in working order. It then becomes the responsibility of the tenant to make sure that the batteries are changed whenever necessary, and that the batteries are in the smoke detector when they leave the unit. I can't tell you how many times tenants have not replaced the batteries. For whatever reason, tenants seem to ignore the fact that the smoke detectors are there for their safety. Oftentimes when I go into a unit, I hear the beep indicating a weak battery, or the smoke detector is open with the battery missing. I just can't understand their lack of attention in this matter.

28) Surrendering the premises. When the lease is up or the time for the tenant to vacate arrives, he does, I hope, leave the unit. He should leave it in the same condition in which he found it.

29) Legal fees. If these fees become necessary to evict or recapture lost funds due to non-payment of rent or damages, they are the responsibility of the tenant.

30) Any additional conditions or changes must be made in writing. Yes, put everything that you can in writing. I make a file for each tenant. Keep good records. You will find this to be important over the course of your investment business.

31) Additional/special conditions. Here I write in such things as particular parking arrangements, the amount of oil in the tank, certain areas that may be off limits for sleeping quarters such as a third floor room without the proper fire escape, any special arrangements for the appliances, or any other special term that may relate to the property.

32) Megan's Law Statement which was discussed previously.

33) Violation of the lease can be cause for eviction with court costs and attorney fees paid.

34) Tenant acknowledgment of having read the lease and agreeing to it. Also, the validity of the lease statement is included at the end before the signatures of the owner and the tenants.

Additionally, I include a space at the bottom of each page for the tenant to place his initials as well.

Next, you'll find some other terms that deserve consideration as far as being included in your lease.

1) The tenant will agree to use the appliances in a safe manner and only for the purposes for which they were intended. This will cover the misuse of the range for example as a "heater", which is dangerous for the tenants in their unit and adjoining units as well. Unnecessary wear on appliances can also become costly.

2) The tenant agrees to give the landlord notice of any defects in the plumbing, fixtures, heater, or air conditioner. Sometimes if you can catch a problem quick enough, it will save you a considerable amount of money, as well as time in the future.

3) The tenant agrees not to install different or additional locks. This will ensure that you have access to the unit in the case of an emergency. I had this problem once. The heaters for the two units in the building were in the basement. The downstairs tenant added a lock to his door and I needed to enter the basement because of a malfunctioning heater. I had to break into the unit in order to get into the basement and resolve the problem.

4) The tenant agrees to permit the landlord to show the apartment to any prospective tenants after the tenant has given notice to move. This is another way of stating one of the terms in my lease.

5) The tenant agrees that if he/she moves before the agreement has ended, that the landlord has the right to enter the unit to decorate and/or remodel the unit. This term will help to cover you if an issue is ever made that the tenant was still actually renting the unit even though he was not physically there.

135

CHAPTER 15

TRUTH IN RENTING

Each State has guidelines that provide information on the responsibilities and the rights of tenants and landlords. Contact the Department of Community Affairs to obtain this information which most likely will be in the form of a booklet. In New Jersey, the booklet is entitled "Truth in Renting". It is required that landlords give a copy of this information to the tenants when they first move in. Often you can obtain a copy locally by contacting your town's Municipal Building or City Hall, specifically the Office of Inspections.

The booklet will give general information on the lease, security deposits, rents, evictions, and maintenance. Concerning the lease, there are differences in your regular apartment lease, the mobile home lease, and some public housing leases. If a tenant breaks the lease prematurely, he could be subject to paying the rent until the lease has expired, or until the landlord has re-

rented the apartment, or if they could prove that constructive eviction has occurred which is an apartment with unlivable conditions.

Security deposits are regulated in that the maximum amount a landlord can collect as a deposit is one and one-half times the monthly rent. The security deposit must be held in an account separate from your regular business account and must be interest-bearing. As stated previously, you must inform the tenant as to where the account is located. You are to refund any interest on the security deposit.

Your state or municipality may have rent control ordinances that will limit and restrict the amount of rental increases. If not, the increases will be at your discretion. This can be a delicate issue for many reasons. Certainly, as a landlord, your cost of doing business will increase because of property taxes, insurance, fees, and repairs. However, raising rents just for the sake of rent increases may present problems that will cost you more than the increase provides. Each of you has to decide what the best way of handling this is. Personally, I very rarely raise rents at the end of the first year if the tenant has decided to renew the lease. If the tenant has been a model renter, then I will not increase the rent. On the other hand, if I have had problems with maintenance and repairs due to the tenant, then an increase is very likely.

I have had situations where my cost of maintaining a unit has risen only slightly over the period of years and a particular tenant has been in the same unit for a number of years. I have not raised the rent because I wanted to keep the tenant. Perhaps a rent increase would not have given them reason to move, but I just felt comfortable with things the way they were.

Most times, at the end of the second year, I will raise rents slightly to keep pace with the increase in costs. Usually my tenants understand that these increases are necessary. I always increase the rents between tenants, in other words when one tenant leaves, I advertise the unit at a higher rent, approximately $25 a month higher.

Your booklet should include information concerning evictions, what you as a landlord can and cannot do forms and notices that need to be given to the tenant and local courthouse, and reasons for eviction.

Other topics that could possibly be addressed include discrimination, property damages, self-help evictions, landlord identity, Senior Citizen provisions, heat and utility requirements, and violations and penalties for failure to adhere to the laws and provisions of your state or municipality.

CHAPTER 16

THE INSPECTION

Your rental unit will need to be inspected by the officials of your municipality. The frequency and costs of these inspections will vary from town to town. Even in our small county there are varying rates and frequency of inspection periods. The largest town in our county charges $55 per unit per year as a registration and inspection fee. The unit needs to be inspected only when the tenants change. The fee is due on the first of each year and increases to $75 if paid after the first.

In my particular town, the fee is also $55 per year due by the first of March. If paid after March first, then it too increases to $75. However, the unit must be inspected each year regardless of whether or not the tenants change.

The inspection form will also vary but contains the basic information such as address, number of units, the owner's name, in-county agent if the owner is living out of the county, telephone numbers in case of an emergency, and the lot and block numbers of the property.

The report also indicates the number of bedrooms in the unit, the legal occupancy that is permitted in each unit, and area to state the "overall appearance" of the unit; good, fair, or poor.

Many, but not all, of the things inspectors are checking for include the following:

1) Smoke detectors. Are they present in the proper location, and are they operating. We discussed these in a previous chapter.

2) Handrails. These are needed on all sets of stairs on the outside entrances, and also on the inside areas such as to the basement and to upper floors.

3) The hot water heater relief valve/floor discharge must be affixed in according to code.

4) Third floor emergency exit. Here, too, codes may differ somewhat. If the third floor area of the unit is to be used as a sleeping area, then a proper emergency exit must be in place. This will include the obvious exterior stairway, and possibly regulated window size and type. I have one unit that has an apartment upstairs and downstairs. The upstairs unit requires an emergency exit on the third floor only because there is a total of three units in the building. The other unit is the other half of a half-double and owned by someone else. According to the code, if there were only two units in the building, the emergency exit would not be necessary; the third unit is the

cause for the exit. Remember to check with the building inspector and code officer in your town.

5) Windows. All windows must be in operating order, able to be opened and closed easily. The local codes may differ concerning sash locks (my units must have these locks installed and in working order). The windows must be glazed properly as well.

6) The heating system must be in working order. The inspector may ask when the heater was serviced. Maintenance is a good preventive measure. Filters are inexpensive and easy to change. There are also requirements that state that the heating system must be able to maintain a certain temperature.

Some of the other general things that the inspectors will want to check include the plumbing fixtures, (checking for drips, leaks and proper installation), screens for the windows, cleanliness of the unit inside and outside, doors, porches, decks, whether the unit needs painting on the interior or exterior, and any evidence of infestation by mice, roaches, or rats.

The inspection may be viewed as an inconvenience, but ultimately it is to your benefit. Before you rent each unit, take pictures and make notes as to the appearance and condition. Each time the inspector checks your unit, he will note any damages. If the tenant has caused the damages, it will be easy to prove. The inspector will be prepared to back you up if needed. Any dangerous conditions that might be noted by the inspector may save you a lot of grief and money down the road. A general rule that I go by is fix any problem as soon as possible, and fix it right. Neglect or patchwork will always come back to haunt me in the future. Many times putting off a problem now results in a much more expensive remedy in the future.

If you ever have a situation where a tenant has done extensive damage to your unit, then it will be helpful to have the last inspection report to use as evidence on your behalf.

Usually you have 30 days to complete any repairs before the re-inspection, if one is required. Any dangerous conditions will have to be completed much sooner. When I have completed the repairs, I notify the inspector in writing as to exactly what was done and when. I do not believe that this step is necessary; it's just something that I do.

If you have to go to court over a particular tenant who may have damaged your property, the inspector may be called as a witness on your behalf.

My dealings with the local inspectors have been good over the years. They know that I try to keep my units as nice as possible, and that I will take care of any necessary repairs in a timely manner. They have always been fair with me, and I respect them for that. I would hope that all inspectors everywhere would be so fair.

CHAPTER 17

HERE COMES THE JUDGE

It would be great if none of you reading this book ever has to go to court on a landlord/tenant matter. That is my hope for you. However, there may be a time when a tenant has to be evicted because of non-payment of rent, causing damage to the unit, or other lease violations. If this happens, there are certain steps that must be followed and forms that must be sent to the tenant and filed with the court before the actual hearing date. Failure to provide proper notification to the tenants may jeopardize your case against them. Failure to be properly prepared for your hearing will have a negative impact on the results that you are hoping for.

The most common reason for eviction is for non-payment of rent. You may seek eviction also for habitual late rent payments by filing and mailing the proper notices to your tenant. In the lease chapter, I stated that if the rent is not paid by the 15th of the month, I begin eviction proceedings. By this I mean that I file the papers with the local court to secure a court date. Failure to pay the rent when it is due requires no written notice to begin legal action. If your tenant is habitually late with the rent payments, send him/her a 'notice to cease' paying the rent late. You must then follow this notice up with a second notice, often called a 'notice to quit'. One month after the second notice, you may begin the eviction process for this cause. Send your notices by regular and certified mail each time so that you have proof that the tenant did actually receive your notice.

Another cause for eviction is if a tenant is disorderly and disturbs the peace of other tenants or neighbors. You may begin eviction three days after the second written notice. If a tenant causes damage to your property, legal action can begin three days after a written notice.

Other reasons for eviction include, but are not limited to, the following:
1) A tenant continues to break rules or terms of the lease
2) If you, the owner, have been cited for violations of state codes, and a) if you want to board up or demolish a property, b) if you cannot fix the violations without removing the tenant, c) if you are seeking to correct illegal occupancy, d) if you are removing the property from the rental market or from residential use, e) if you are converting your property to a condominium.

Each reason for eviction carries a procedure and varying forms of notification. Check with your own state to obtain this information.

Once the proper forms and notices are followed, you will be scheduled for a court date if you have not resolved the situation in the meantime. My limited experience with the local court system has found that to obtain a court date takes two to three weeks from the time that I file the papers. The first time that I had to go to court over a landlord/tenant problem, I was quite nervous and anxious about the situation. I hadn't been to court other than serving as a juror. I imagined thousands of people watching me, riding on my every word, as I pleaded my case before the judge. My preconceived ideas were not quite like reality.

In our local area, all landlord/tenant and small claims cases are heard on the same day. All cases are to report to the courthouse at 9am, and people are jam packed like sardines. The judge would give a little talk at the beginning to everyone present saying that time was a factor, so it was in everyone's best interest to try and resolve the cases as soon as possible. If the cases weren't resolved by a particular time, then the parties would have to return another day. Each party, the landlord and the tenant, was encouraged to "give a little, or to compromise" to help resolve the issue. I always took exception with this because if rent was due, then rent was due, and I did not feel that I should compromise about that.

All of the cases scheduled for that day were read. If the plaintiff (the landlord seeking rent or eviction), did not show up, the case was dismissed. If the defendant did not show, then judgment was entered in the landlord's favor.

A note here about having a tenant evicted for non-payment or any other reason: In addition to the eviction cause, you need to file for possession at the same time. This means that if the tenant does not come up with the rent due, then after three days, you gain possession of the property. If you do not do this at the same time that you file for eviction, you will have to go back to court to get possession of the property if the tenant fails to move out voluntarily.

If both parties are present for the case, it is so noted, and once the entire list is read, the judge goes back to the beginning of the list. The judge will hear the cases first where an attorney representing one of the parties is present. If neither party has an attorney present, then the case is referred to a court-appointed mediator, who is an attorney, or someone who is studying to be an attorney. The two parties sit down with this mediator and try to come to an understanding, compromise, or solution. If an agreement is made with the mediator, the agreement form is signed by both parties, and then each party is bound to the terms of the agreement (pay all the rent, part of the rent, etc).

If an agreement cannot be reached, the parties return to court and await the hearing before the judge.

Always be prepared with as much documentation to support your case as possible. Take receipts, leases, inspection reports, and especially pictures of any damage that may have been caused. Take copies of any and all notices that you have sent to the tenant. If you have hired an attorney to represent you, he/she will have asked you for copies of any documentation. I have always represented myself in cases. However, there were times when I wished that I had used an attorney. A general rule might be that if you need to get the tenant out immediately or if there is a large amount of money at stake, seek the representation of an attorney. If, on the other hand, the matter is relatively small (a couple of hundred dollars) you probably can handle the situation yourself if you are prepared.

As I mentioned previously, procedure may vary from location to location. Become familiar with the legal procedures in your area. The staff at the courthouse can be a big help in explaining the workings of the system and can provide you with the forms to file for your particular case.

You don't always get your money. It is worth the time though, to obtain the judgment, and, if necessary, to secure a wage execution to recover any money due to you. For an extra fee, you can have the judgment recorded with the Superior Court. Any time in the future that the tenant attempts to buy or sell property, the Superior Court record will indicate the judgment and the amount due to you. This amount must be paid before the property transaction can take place. You will get your money in this instance.

If, for some reason, your tenant has 'skipped out' and you are unable to locate him, rely on the information on the application for names of friends, relatives, employers, social security numbers, and driver's license numbers to assist you in locating the lost tenant.

CHAPTER 18

ODDS AND ENDS

This chapter is meant to touch upon some miscellaneous topics that perhaps do not require an entire chapter but, nonetheless, need mentioning. I hope that you will find a "nugget" or two in this chapter as well.

INSURANCE

Insurance is one of those dreaded necessities. We hope that we never have to use our insurance, for if we do, it means that we have had considerable damage occur or that we have a claim for either fire or liability. In the twenty years that I have been in the investment business, I have never had a claim against me, or my property. You should all be so fortunate.

When I think back to all of the thousands of dollars that I have paid in premiums over the years, it's a tough lump to swallow. However, if a claim had been filed, there is a good chance that the claim amount would have exceeded the total in premiums that have been paid. So, in that vein, it becomes easier to justify all of the premiums.

It is very important to have your property covered in the event of fire or liability. One stray spark could cause you to lose a fortune if you do not have adequate coverage. Or, if a tenant or guest were injured at the rental property, your liability insurance would provide coverage if necessary.

As far as fire insurance goes, most companies want to cover the unit for the amount that would be needed to replace the property. In most cases this amount is sufficient because your market value will probably be less than replacement costs. Concerning liability insurance, I would suggest the maximum amount of coverage that you feel you can comfortably afford.

In times past, you would make a phone call, the agent would take a picture of the property and maybe walk through the inside, then write the policy. With each passing year, insurance companies are making it tougher and tougher to get the coverage on investment properties. If the property has any old wiring still in use, the insurance company may make you replace it before you can get coverage. Cracked or raised sidewalks are another issue. You may have to have them repaired before or shortly after you purchase the property to avoid the chance of someone tripping and filing a lawsuit. Handrails for all steps, (entrance, second floor, attic, and basement), are required.

Most recently, properties with underground oil storage tanks have become subject to testing and certification before insurance is granted. This is a matter that you should check into before you purchase a property. Know what your insurance company's position and requirements are concerning this matter.

If you are purchasing a real 'fixer upper', you may have a difficult time finding a company to insure you until all of the repairs are made. If this is the case, some companies offer interim insurance through construction or builder's risk policies.

A final note on insurance, to quote an 'oldie but goodie', "my mama told me, you better shop around"! Take time and effort to compare prices and coverage from company to company. Investigate the company as much as possible to insure that it is a reputable company. Even a small difference of a couple of dollars a month will, over time, add up to considerable savings.

RENT INCREASES

Increasing the rents is a subject that deserves careful consideration. Over the years, your costs, such as insurance, taxes, utilities, and fees, will undoubtedly rise. Your rents will have to reflect those increases. All landlords are in the same boat on this issue of increased expenses. The question is, do you raise your rents each and every year? How much do you increase the rents? Will tenants be offended and move out?

The answers to these questions will vary with each individual landlord. As I mentioned in a previous chapter, I do not raise rents every year. Some landlords do, and if it works for them, great. I wonder what percentage of tenants move away because of the increase. Remember, if you lose only one month's rent because of a vacancy due to a tenant moving out because of a rent increase, it will take quite a considerable time (perhaps more than a year) to make up the lost money with higher rents.

However, there are times that rent increases are unavoidable and justified, and part of the way things are. If I have a tenant to whom I really don't want to renew, the increased rent is substantial, and the notice is sent with pleasure. If he wants to pay the higher rent, fine, as long as he has been abiding by the other terms of the lease. If he decides to move out, that's okay too.

I do raise the rents each time a tenant moves out of an apartment. Depending on the unit, I may raise rents $20 to $25 per month. Don't forget to keep an eye on your competition, making sure that your rents are not too far out of line with comparable units in your area. Some municipalities may have rent control provisions that may affect the amount of rent that can be charged. Check in advance for any such regulations in the area in which you intend to purchase investment properties.

For my good tenants, I try very hard not to raise rents when they sign up for the second year. If they have paid their rents on time and kept the property in good condition, then I will do whatever I can to keep the rent at the same level for the second year. At the beginning of the third year, I usually increase the rents slightly, perhaps $20 or so, depending on the unit. Tenants usually understand that your costs as a landlord are increasing and are willing to pay the increase, provided it is reasonable.

If you have tenants who are on the section 8 program, the government will determine the increases which are minimum, or, on occasion, not at all. You must request this increase each year in writing, with the reasons to justify the increase, namely higher taxes, increased insurance, or other.

NEGOTIATIONS

Negotiating the selling price of a property that you are interested in can be challenging, exciting, rewarding, profitable, and sometimes nerve-wracking. Or it could be just plain uneventful. Each situation will be completely different, with all kinds of variables to consider. Some of these variables will include, but are not limited to, the area, length of time the property has been on the market, the condition of the property, market value, comparable sales of similar properties in the same area, and the seller himself.

Area, condition, and comparable properties in a particular area will give you a good idea of the market value of the property that you are interested in. These are 'tangible' variables that are in black and white and ones that you can see with your own eyes. These variables can be argued and debated, but realistically, you can't hide the condition or pretend that the property is in an area other than the one it is in. When you attempt to get a mortgage on this investment property, the bank will appraise the property using sales of similar properties in that particular neighborhood. If the property that you are interested in does not appraise up to the selling price, the bank will ask you to come up with the difference or the seller may need to adjust the selling price, or you may not be given the mortgage. This is something that you need to remember when you try to sell this property at some point in the future. If you put a substantial amount of your own money into a property in order to obtain a mortgage, keep in mind that unless the market changes drastically in your favor by the time that you are ready to sell, the new buyers will be having the same problem. They will have a difficult time obtaining a mortgage to buy the property from you.

The 'intangible' variable is the seller. Does the seller need to sell? Is he in any hurry? Is this a property that the sellers will do anything to get rid of? Is the property being sold as a part of a divorce settlement? Is the owner alive, or is this part of an estate sale? These are all questions that could make a difference, sometimes substantially, as to the selling price and your final negotiated price. Obviously, the more anxious the seller is, the better for you. These are "motivated sellers", and usually they will try to negotiate any reasonable offer to get them out from under the property. For whatever reason or reasons, they want to sell as soon as possible.

So how do you know what the particular situation is? For starters, you could ask. Sometimes the seller will tell you the situation, sometimes in detail, sometimes generally speaking. Be a good listener and try to ascertain the real reasons that the seller wants to unload the property.

One of the rental properties that I purchased was a single home. The real estate agent came across my name and number, gave me a call, and proceeded to tell me that someone had given her my name as one who purchased rental properties. After I confirmed that fact, she told me of a single house that was for sale for $55,000 and asked if I would take a ride past the property. In my head, I was doing some quick math and figured that this property would not generate much if any cash flow, but as a courtesy I said that I would, indeed, look at the property. Ten minutes later, the owner of this property called me. She said that she didn't know what price the agent gave me, but she, (the owner) would be willing to sell the house for $30 to $35,000! Suddenly, the math seemed to work out much better! At that price, there would be a positive cash flow. I now definitely had to see the house and what kind of condition it was in.

Once I arrived at the property, I found that the house was in fairly good condition. There had been many updates (roof, plumbing, heating, and electric). Inside it was in need of cosmetic work, but nothing major. As I walked through the property, the seller just came out and told me why she wanted to sell. Extended family members, whom she really wanted out, had been living there and the property had been on the market for some time. She basically came out and told me that she was willing to do whatever necessary to sell the house.

The next day, I called the agent, offered $30,000 with $10,000 down, and asked the seller to hold a mortgage for the difference. Twenty minutes later we were signing the papers. I thought that I had a good deal, but I couldn't help but think what the bottom price could have been. She accepted my offer so quickly, that maybe she would have taken a lower price! Oh well, I was content with my offer or I wouldn't have made it in the first place. Don't fret over what might have been.

The process was made even sweeter a year or so into the mortgage. The seller informed me that she was selling the mortgage to another company. I knew that the mortgage would have to be discounted somewhat in order for her to sell, so I just came out and asked her how much did she have to discount the amount due for the other company to purchase it. She told me that it was about $ 2,500. Fortunately I had completed another settlement a few days earlier, and I had some cash available. I then asked if she would accept the discounted amount from me as payment in full (since she would be giving that money to the other company anyway), and she agreed. So, I was able to save $ 2,500. The deal worked out well as a rental for years, and then I sold the property to the tenant for 60,000.

The point here is, ask as many questions as possible, not only listening, but understanding the situation at hand. Don't be afraid to offer a lower price than the asking price. A good practice is to offer slightly lower than the price that you will actually be willing to pay. The seller may say, yes, no, or no, but. If your offer is unreasonable, you may not even get an answer back as the buyer will consider you unrealistic and not give you the time of day. If your offer is close to the bottom line of the seller, you will, in most cases, get a counter offer from the seller. If the seller thinks that your offer is one that might be the best he can get and he is not a haggler, then you may just get the property for your initial offer. Be bold enough to make an offer that might be considerably lower than the selling price. Every thousand dollars that you save now will, over years, be realized as a savings of many thousands of dollars.

I mentioned in the introduction that I spent 18 years in the retail furniture business. Some furniture stores sell furniture for the marked price only. Don't ask for discounts because the owners or managers will say no. They say pay the price that is marked or you can go elsewhere. Some home sellers are like that as well. It may be that they are hard-nosed, and you insult their pride with a lower offer. It could be that they have to have the asking price to pay off all the bills, etc. You never know, unless, of course, they tell you.

The particular store that I worked for was open to offers, cash discounts, creative financing, whatever. That was just the way that we operated. For example, if we had a three-piece living room set marked at $1,000, we would have some customers come in, like the set, and pay the $1,000 without asking about any discount or special deal. The next customer would come in, fall in love with the same set, and say that he would pay only $850 for the three pieces. The customer would ask us to sell the furniture for $850 or he would go to another store. As manager, I was authorized to make many decisions on my own, but if the owner was present, I would confer with him about the offer. Our concerns varied from how much did the set cost, how long have we had the set (was it something that had been around for a long time?), and sometimes the decision was influenced by whether or not we needed money to pay a particular bill on that day. Usually, the answer to a reasonable offer was "yes". We did not want to lose a sale to a competitor, nor let needed cash slip through our hands. On occasion, the answer was "no", but we would sell it for, say, $900. This way the customer still received a discount they were happy about, and we still made the sale.

At other times we would have customers come into the store and offer an unreasonable amount. When we said "no", the customer either walked out the door, or came back with a higher offer. The offer might have been $500 for the same three-piece set. How dare the customer insult us! Many times the owner would tell me not even to bother with such a customer because they were being ridiculous. I must confess, though, there were days that the offer of $500 would have been accepted given the right circumstances.

Sometimes I would encounter a buyer who would make an offer and say "this is the final offer---take it or leave it!" There were times when the buyer actually meant what they said, but there were also other times when we would refuse the offer only to have the buyer come back with another offer that was acceptable. As a real estate agent I encounter the same thing when buyers and sellers say to me and to each other that the particular offer or counter offer is the best and final offer that will be presented. Again, sometimes that would be true, but more often than not one party or the other would concede to a point.

Negotiating over furniture aided me in my future endeavors with the investment properties. There will be times that you won't get the answer that you want. You need to decide how badly you want the property, and will it be a good investment. Try not to get too involved personally. If your initial offer is rejected, don't be afraid to come back with another offer, even if the seller told you that you were crazy. In some cases, I try to make a case for my offer (condition, marketability, cash flow). This may or may not be a help. It depends again on how much the seller is willing to listen, and how badly he wants to get rid of the property.

This process is a cat-and-mouse game. Each situation is different. My overall, general advice is to find out as much as possible concerning the seller's position and value of comparable property. Be fair, but work for the best possible price.

One last note concerning properties that already have tenants: Tenants have certain rights concerning their tenancy in properties after they have been sold. Be clear as to these rights, when their lease is up, what kind of tenants they are, what is the rental payment history, and what, if any, problems should be brought to your attention. If the unit that you are buying has problem tenants, make it the responsibility of the sellers to have the tenants evicted BEFORE you purchase that property.

GOALS AND STRATEGIES

The 'process' of investing in income properties will lead each of you to different goals, strategies, and levels of success. As stated previously, get into the business with a specific goal in mind. This is not to say that your goal cannot be changed or adjusted. Do you want to own one property, five, ten, or one hundred? Do you want this business to supply some extra income, be the means for paying for weddings, college educations, or gifts to your children, or be the business to be your vehicle for retirement?

As you begin the 'process' you will soon find your likes and dislikes, your strengths and weaknesses, and your level of interest and desire. If you find that this is a business that you can tolerate, or even enjoy, the sky is the limit. The personal satisfaction that you gain from the challenges, and the profits that you will realize, will fuel you to accomplishing your desired goals.

Some of your management goals might be to: a) attract good tenants with nice, affordable housing, keep these good tenants whenever possible by maintaining the unit and keeping reasonable rents, b) keeping the vacancy rate as low as possible because an empty apartment pays no rent, but demands that the mortgage, taxes, insurance, and utility bills continue to be paid. Time is one thing that can never be made up. A month lost to vacancy will never be retrieved. We also need to keep a good balance between keeping the rents reasonable and getting the most that we can in rent for each unit. Your particular area and neighborhood and the rate of tenant turnover will be your guiding factors in this concern. And, certainly, we want to encourage each tenant to pay on time every time.

Once you own property, the question of how long to hold on to that property will surface sooner or later. I, personally, do not have any set rule to go by. One or two years, or ten to twenty years could be the time that I hold onto a particular property. I have had some properties that run smoothly with a minimum of tenant turnover. I could keep these almost forever. I say almost because I will hang on to them as long as I am in the business. When I first started, I did not envision that the investment business was something I was going to do for the rest of my life. It was a means to achieve the financial goals I had in mind. I could see myself at the end of a specified time selling off all of the properties and retiring into some other venture or to my lakeside home. The low turnover, hassle-free (almost), properties will make your investing enjoyable.

There are other properties that will be 'marginal' for you. Those are the ones that you could keep or you could sell at any time. If you have paid as much as you can on principal, these will yield a nice profit only a few years or so after you have purchased them. Within ten years, you will have accumulated a substantial amount of equity, and these properties could be the springboard to other bigger, or more profitable, investments.

Finally, you may have a property that you simply do not want anymore, even if you just purchased it within a year or so. Or it may have been a property that was good for a while and all of a sudden you are having problems with your tenants, or neighbors, or repairs. You just want to sell it for whatever reason. If you see this happening to one of your properties, my advice would be to sell it as soon as possible. If you have to sell it without a profit, do it, especially if you know that the problems won't correct themselves. I have had a couple of properties in neighborhoods that were not too bad until other landlords put terrible tenants in the adjoining or nearby properties. I lost several good tenants because of disruptive tenants in other units. Unless the other landlord has a change of heart, you will have an ongoing problem.

I have had tenants who lived in my units for a long period of time and decided that they would like to buy the house from me. There have been times when I have had those properties paid off, or paid down, to a point where I could do some creative financing and turn around and sell the units to the tenants themselves. This was mutually beneficial because the tenants did not have to move out, and they could purchase the property directly from me without incurring a few thousand dollars in bank fees to obtain a mortgage. Now my investment was in the form of interest each month without the concerns or headaches of being a landlord. It is a good investment, and something that you might consider once you have been investing for awhile.

I also mentioned that I buy properties strictly for the short-term as well. Usually these are properties that need much cosmetic or even extensive work. They are priced low enough for me to purchase, renovate, and then re-sell and make a decent profit. These projects help the cash flow along over the years.

Don't get emotionally attached to your properties. Make good, sound business decisions concerning the length of time that you are to keep each unit.

When you have decided to sell, make the effort to make your property as attractive as possible. This will add value and attract investors who might otherwise not look at your property. Remember the impressions that you had when you viewed prospective properties. We all want properties to look nice and attractive, and we are all turned off by dirt, clutter, holes in the wall, torn carpet, etc. I know that it is difficult sometimes to 'spruce up the unit when you have tenants still living in there. Try to do what you can within reason.

Repair anything that will jump out screaming "fix me, fix me"! to you or another potential investor. Most investors can look past the personal belongings of tenants as long as they are not filthy or too cluttered. Most of the time investors want to purchase the property already rented out to tenants. This will give them immediate cash flow upon closing.

CHAPTER 19

TO BE OR NOT TO BE

This is the question that we all must answer. Do I want to be a landlord or not? Here is where I usually give my pep talk. Not everyone is cut out to be a landlord. But you will never know for sure unless you try. The worst that can happen is that you re-sell your investment property, make a little bit of money, and become wiser for the experience. The upside potential is tremendous. You may find that you love the business, the people, the financial freedom that will come with continued investment, and the challenges of obtaining properties in various ways.

"Nothing ventured, nothing gained" is appropriate for this business as well. When you do venture, the "BIG D's" come into play. The "BIG D's" are DESIRE, DEDICATION, AND DETERMINATION.

You must initially have the *DESIRE* to become a landlord, and that has to be followed with the desire to be the best landlord possible. Always treat your tenants fairly, and they will usually respond in like manner. Desire to have the best possible units. You should have a desire to succeed. Set your goals when you start out. Once you are in the business, there is nothing wrong with adjusting and altering those goals to accommodate the needs and direction you want to work toward.

DEDICATION. One of the quotes that I have posted on my wall states *"In the final analysis, the success or failure of a vision depends on the strength of the commitment behind it"*. The author is unknown to me, but this has been an inspiration to me over the years. If you are not dedicated to the rental business, you will find it difficult to maintain the level of commitment that will benefit you the most. If you become an absentee landlord, your tenants and your properties will reflect your lack of concern. This will reap problems for you that will eventually force you out of the business, perhaps at a loss or a level substantially less than you first envisioned. You may become totally hardened to the needs of tenants, neighbors, and your property. Landlords who care only about the rent that comes in and not about the people to whom they rent, or what happens to their properties, are the cause of problems for neighbors, the community, and themselves. We call them slumlords. The slumlord gives the conscientious landlord a bad name. Most of the time they don't even care that they give you a bad name.

Be a good landlord! You will attract better tenants. Believe me, word spreads. If you are a good landlord, your reputation will do much to attract good tenants. Likewise, if you become a slumlord, you will attract only the tenants who can't find any place else to rent. Being a good landlord will cause you and your tenants to be at peace with the neighbors, will earn you the respect of the city officials who inspect your properties, and will go a long way in helping you to sleep better at night.

The final "D", *DETERMINATION,* is the staying power you need to succeed and reach your goal whether it is for one income property, ten, or one hundred. It is also the staying power to help you through the tough times, and there will be tough times. If I hadn't been determined, I would have given up after the first investment property. The first for me was a killer, the second was pretty tough too, but after that, things started to run more smoothly. If I had quit after the first or second, I would not be writing this book.

I am still working toward my initial goal. The wealth that I have accumulated as a result of the investment business is enough to provide my three daughters with a college education, marry them off, and allow my wife and me to retire without having to worry about whether or not social security will be sufficient or even available by the time we reach those golden years.

I trust that my stated objectives will be realized by you. This book is unlike most books that I have read on the subject of investment properties. Most concentrate on the millions of dollars that are there for the taking. I do not doubt that there are many success stories as a result of those books.

Certainly, millions of dollars is an attainable goal in this business. I have not belabored the fact that millions of dollars can be attained if that is your goal. Nor have I continually 'pumped you up', hammering at all the positives and glorious benefits of being a landlord and investor in income properties. I wanted to give you the basics that you will need to get off on the right foot, basics that will save you a substantial amount of money since you know what to look for beforehand.

I have tried in this book to give you the "nitty gritty", the "trench notes" reality and "hands on problems" that are associated with the investment business. These are not normally the things that sell books or attract hopeful investors. When I started in the investment business I knew next to nothing about it, and ninety percent of the information that I have shared with you in these pages is information and experience that I have gained since getting into the business. It is information that I would have been very grateful to have had when I first started. My hope is that you will have found it valuable to you as you begin your journey, your "process" towards financial security. Have a prosperous journey!

ADDITIONAL FORMS

TENANT SECURITY / CLEANING DEPOSIT TRANSACTIONS

TENANT TRACKING FORM

NOTICE TO TERMINATE LEASE

NOTICE TO CEASE

RENT INCREASE NOTICE

TENANT SECURITY/ CLEANING DEPOSIT
TRANSACTIONS

As specified in the lease agreement, the security/cleaning deposit shall be refunded not more than 30 days after the tenants have moved out and returned their keys. Any past due rent, late charges or amounts for damages and/or cleaning will be deducted from the security deposit.

Any amount remaining and due to the tenant will be sent to the address stated at the bottom of this page. If the security/cleaning deposit is insufficient to cover the charges mentioned above, the tenant shall be liable, and shall forward the payment to the landlord within ten (10) days of receipt of this form.

Property Address:

_____

Tenant Name:

_____

Date of Lease:

_____

Date Dwelling was Vacated:

_____

Amount of Security Deposit:

_____

Earned Accumulated Interest:

_____

Total Amount of Security:

_____

Deductions:

    1. Past due rent _____

    2. Late Charges _____

    3. Cleaning Fee _____

    4. Damages/repairs _____*

    5. Other _____**

Total Deductions _____

Amount Refunded _____

Amount due and owing from tenant

_____

Tenant's Forwarding Address:

_____

Phone number where tenant can be reached

_____

*Detail damages/ repairs if necessary...**Detail other if necessary

_____

LANDLORD   DATE

TENANT TRACKING FORM

Tenant Name

_____

Property Address

_____

Move-In Date _____

Beginning Rent _____

Move-Out Date _____

Ending Rent _____

Rent paid on time?

_____

Would I re-rent to this tenant at some future time?

_____

Was the 60-Day Notice given in writing?

_____

Dwelling in good condition upon departure?

_____

Reason for Leaving?

_____

_____

Total Security/cleaning deposit

_____

Amount of Deposit refunded

_____

Amount due and owing by tenant

_____

Were all amounts due paid?

_____

_____

LANDLORD   DATE

NOTICE TO TERMINATE LEASE

<u>TO:</u> John Tenant and Mary Tenant, husband and wife, Tenant(s).

You now rent the dwelling known as

_____,

in the city of_____,

in the state of_____.

Termination of Lease. Your lease which was dated_____, will be

terminated as of_____.

You must leave and vacate this property on or before the termination date.

Your lease is being terminated because

_____

_____

_____

_____

_____

You must move out and have delivered possession to me, the landlord, by the

date of termination.

_____

LANDLORD   DATE

NOTICE TO CEASE

<u>TO:</u> John Tenant, and Mary Tenant, husband and wife, Tenant(s).

You now rent the dwelling known as

_____,

in the city of_____,

in the state of_____.

    Please read this *NOTICE TO CEASE* very carefully. You must immediately cease the following acts that violate the terms of the lease agreement. If you fail to cease these acts, you will be evicted from your dwelling. This means that you will be forced to vacate the dwelling. Your eviction is being considered for the following reasons:

_____

_____

_____

_____

_____

(These reasons include non-payment of rent, habitual late rent payments, disturbances, damages, or other violations of the lease)

_____

LANDLORD   DATE

RENT INCREASE NOTICE

<u>TO:</u> John Tenant and Mary Tenant, husband and wife, Tenant(s).

Present Address:

_____

_____

Current Rent Amount: _____

Reason for this Notice: The owners want to increase the rent for this dwelling unit. In order to increase the rent, your present lease, which is dated_____, must be terminated, and a new lease offered at the new, increased rent. The owner may also make other changes to your lease, which will be noted under "other changes".

Termination of Present Lease. Your present lease will be terminated as of_____.

This means that you must quit and surrender the property by this date unless you have agreed to the increased rent amount.

New Rent. You may rent this property as of

_____, for the amount of

_____per month. Your rent remains due on the first day of each month thereafter.

Other Changes. (For example, term of lease or the amount now required for the security deposit)

_____

_____

_____

_____

_____

Acceptance. If you have remained in the rental dwelling after the date of termination, it will mean that you have accepted the new rent amount as well as the other changes to your lease.

_____

LANDLORD   DATE

ABOUT THE AUTHOR

Sam Siligato obtained an Associate's degree from Cumberland County College and a Bachelor's degree from Rowan University, both in New Jersey. Before he ventured into real estate, Sam taught secondary school for six years and managed a retail furniture store for eighteen years. Sam has been a real estate investor and landlord for twenty-one years and held a real estate license in the State of New Jersey for twenty-three years. He lives with his wife of twenty-eight years and has three daughters.